For the last four dec[ades Phil has been a] mentor, both in the [personal and business] relationship with Phil, which goes back almost 40 years, has changed my life. Even after his retirement from Northwestern Mutual, I continue to turn to him for counsel, guidance and advice. His ability to bring out the best in the people he works with is a pure blessing not only for Phil, but for the people he has been associated with through out the years.

Phillip J. Pierz has made a difference in my life. His management skills, his friendship and most of all his loyalty, have made and will continue to make a difference in my life.
　　　　　　　–Vincent Auriemma, CLU ChFC (Of the tens
　　　　　　　　of thousands of financial representatives,
　　　　　　　　　Vinny has ranked 48th in the history of
　　　　　　　　Northwestern Mutual Financial Network)

Intuitive, compassionate and empathetic in all his dealings with his "clients," defined as those of us who were fortunate enough to be under his guidance, Phil's greatest lesson to me is this: "See people as they can be, not as they are." That advice has served me well over the years, in every aspect of my life. Thanks Phil!
　　　　　　　　　–Hunter Stollman CLC ChFC CFP
　　　(Inspiration to all for tenaciously surmounting life-threat-
　　　　ening illness to remain a consistent top producer in the
　　　　　　　　Northwestern Mutual Financial Network)

What can I say? I owe my life to Phil. His help with my management skills goes without saying. I've been with Shoff Darby Companies, Inc. since the very beginning and Phil has helped me become a better leader, conscientious worker and what he always calls me – "the soul" of the organization. Without his help this would never have happened. All of his training has made me a better person and made my personal life a breeze. Best of luck with this wonderful book.
　　　　　　　　　–Pat Graf, Co-Vice Chairman, Shoff
　　　　　　　　　Darby Insurance Companies, Inc.

The quintessential path to thinking outside the box. A completely original and groundbreaking philosophy on sales management will render the conventional thinking obsolete. Mr. Pierz has delineated, in an extraordinary and powerful manner, the development of a successful new-era sales manager.
>   –Art Jacobson, CEO EG Partners, Founder, former Owner and CEO of Olympic Manufacturing Co. Inc.

Phil Pierz is a leader's leader and a trainer's trainer. I've had the great pleasure in knowing Phil for over 60 years. We went to grammar school and high school together in Brooklyn, NY. I joined his NML agency in 1972 and we started Shoff Darby Co., a property and casualty company, from scratch in 1973. Today, it is one of the largest independent agencies in CT. He has engineered the building of not one, but two companies from nothing to what they are today.

In 1971, his General Agency for Northwestern Mutual was formed and not many years later, was in the top ten every year and remained there until his retirement in October 2002. He achieved the same astounding results with the Shoff Darby Insurance Companies in the Property and Casualty industry by using the same training techniques and adapting them. This is an opportunity for agencies throughout the county to gain tremendous advantage in all business endeavors.
>   –Robert P. Latkany, CLC CASL CLTC (Co-Founder with Phil of Shoff Darby Insurance Companies, Inc.)

Phil's outstanding success in management reflects his intelligence, warmth, wit and honesty. He teaches and supports those who work for him, has faith in their ability to succeed, and is loyal to them and their families over the long haul. This book provides valuable insights into how to build a successful business.
>   –George Keane, President Emeritus, Commonfund Group

TAKING THE HIGH ROAD
TO THE BOTTOM LINE

22 Principles for Success in Building
and Maintaining a Dynamic Sales Force

Phillip J. Pierz
with Jennifer A. Stern

Copyright © 2008 Phillip J. Pierz with Jennifer A. Stern
All rights reserved.

ISBN: 1-4196-8970-3
ISBN-13: 9781419689703

Visit www.booksurge.com to order additional copies.

TAKING THE HIGH ROAD TO THE BOTTOM LINE

Phillip J. Pierz
with Jennifer A. Stern

To my wonderful, incredible wife, Marcia,
who by the way she lives and loves, brings
out the best in people, especially me

ACKNOWLEDGEMENTS

Acknowledgements and thank-you to my dear and talented daughter, Jennifer A. Stern, for her two years of interviewing me and for so insightfully and professionally putting into print my lifetime's deeply felt perspectives, commitments and responsibilities through my Principles.

And to Don Iodice, one of my dearest and oldest friends, for his important contribution to this manuscript. Knowing my management "Pillars" by having personally experienced them, he interjected my style and tone throughout, thus providing the reader a closer experience of me.

And to the hundreds of agents I have personally trained and supervised and the thousands of sales people that I have been a part of through my tapes and seminars, I salute you as my heroes!

TABLE OF CONTENTS

Principle 1	The Salesperson Is My CLIENT	1
Principle 2	Facilitate Responsibility	5
Principle 3	Be Present	9
Principle 4	Be Gracious	13
Principle 5	Respect Your Representative's Efforts to "Grow Up"	19
Principle 6	Don't Neglect Your Best	23
Principle 7	Make "Helping Others" Part of Your Culture	27
Principle 8	Make Your Producers Your RECRUITERS	31
Principle 9	Be Honest with Potential Recruits	35
Principle 10	Be Involved in Basic Training	41
Principle 11	See People as They CAN Be	47
Principle 12	Special Situations Deserve Special Attention	51
Principle 13	Learn What Motivates Each Salesperson and Teach Him or Her How to Use It	59
Principle 14	Set Up Incentive Programs that Are WIN-WIN	65

Principle 15	Select Future Managers Based on WHAT THEY STAND FOR	69
Principle 16	You Have No Idea of the Impact of What YOU DO and SAY	73
Principle 17	Avoid Triangular Relationships (Like the Plague)	79
Principle 18	Get the Monkeys Off Your Back	83
Principle 19	Set ATTAINABLE GOALS as an Organization	89
Principle 20	Have NO SECRETS Among Management	95
Principle 21	Management Should Work by CONSENSUS	99
Principle 22	Management Meetings Are SACRED	105
	TRANSFERABILITY	109
	AFTERWORD	111
	AUTHOR'S NOTE	113

NURTURING AND GROWING A DYNAMIC SALES FORCE

It's one thing to want to be successful and to strive to do your best. It is quite another thing to enjoy the process of getting there. It's one thing to build a sales organization made up of top producers. It's another to create an environment where all parties, management, sales representatives, and staff, feel supported and well equipped to do their jobs. An environment wherein everyone knows that he or she can find whatever help is needed. And, where each person knows that his and her efforts are appreciated. Where those who are part of it never hesitate to recommend that same opportunity to qualified friends and family members.

In too many businesses today morale and job satisfaction seem to be sacrificed on the altar of high profits. I want you to know that a business can create an atmosphere of high morale and personal satisfaction and still be very profitable. Some managers believe that fear and competition are the best motivators. They believe that a company can't be successful if the employees and associates are enjoying their jobs; or if they themselves like going to work. But, success and happiness need not be incompatible. I truly believe, and have proven, that creating a work environment—a company culture—where you enjoy what you are doing, and where everyone works hard, but also gets adequate support from management and from each other, produces "success which sustains itself." That type of environment fosters sales representatives who produce excellent results and don't burn out. And, perhaps most important, management that looks forward to being at work every day.

Let me tell you a little about myself. When I started on this journey of building a career in sales management, I was as frightened and apprehensive as anyone else. Probably not unlike you, the reader. But, I was also excited and challenged. And committed to the principles I will outline in this book. Principles that I have adhered to not only in growing a sales force but also in the way I lead my life. Principles which have brought me joy and gratification in my career and in my personal, non-business life. What I've done has worked and these principles continue to work. I want to help you achieve the kind of unique success I have enjoyed in developing one of the largest and most successful life insurance sales force in the United States.

I signed on as a life insurance agent representing the Northwestern Mutual Life Insurance Company upon graduating from Georgetown University in 1959. As a result of numerous on-campus recruiting interviews with various life insurance companies (I was a bit of an interview addict), I learned that, despite the industry's poor image, these companies were marketing a truly moral product. A product that could protect families in their most desperate times. In fact, we in Fairfield County, Connecticut, where our agency is located, lived that reality after Sept. 11, 2001. Our associates delivered millions of dollars of death benefits to families who lost loved ones. I also realized that the structure of the life insurance business—where the sales people are essentially independent operators who are compensated solely on a commission basis—would well suit a maverick like me. At that time, and it is still true today, Northwestern agents were the most productive sales people in the life insurance business. Since I wanted to be the best, I joined the Northwestern Mutual agency in Washington, D.C.

After passing all my licensing tests and becoming an agent, I decided that I would become a member of the Million Dollar Round Table (MDRT) in my first year in the business. The MDRT is a prestigious industry-wide organization that requires a certain level of production in order to qualify for membership. There were just three obstacles: my fear of the telephone, my fear of talking to older, mature people, and my fear of public speaking. But I had set a goal and I could not let these fears stand in my way. I enrolled in a twelve-week Dale Carnegie course and I took every opportunity to speak before a group. The phone is a necessary part of any sales representative's business, so I developed a telephone technique that is still used in company-wide training today. By the end of the year I had become the youngest agent ever to qualify for membership in the MDRT.

My introduction to management came in 1965 under the tutelage of the man I consider my mentor, William H. Griffin. Bill was the Northwestern Mutual general agent in Hartford, Conn., and I became his agency supervisor for one year. In 1966 I got my first true management assignment: to run Bill's district office in Stamford, Conn.

In the Northwestern Mutual system, a typical district office is geographically removed from the general agency and is substantially smaller in size. The office I took charge of was made up of a less-than-illustrious group of four agents. Nevertheless, it was an opportunity for me to put my developing ideas and principles to work. By 1971 we had grown our agency to 20 agents plus staff and we had become the number one district agency in Northwestern production. In five years we had progressed from a non-entity to number one. My principles and practices were working.

I found 1971 a wonderful year and a difficult year. Wonderful because Northwestern converted our district agency into a general agency. Difficult because we went from being number one to being to being 68th among all general agencies. Now it truly was time to put my beliefs and principles to work. And go to work we did. Our general agency became one of the top 10 in the company out of more than 100; and we stayed in the top 10 for over 20 years. We peaked at number two in the company; far exceeding our market opportunity designation. By the turn of the century our agency was comprised of five district offices and a total of 115 sales representatives. Yes, these principles do work!

Our businesses succeed only if our associates succeed. Our associates have excelled in every measure of success that our industry offers. Our agency was the first in the world to have more than 50 members in the MDRT, which recognizes the industry's top producers. We had the highest percentage of agents receiving the National Association of Insurance and Financial Advisors National Quality Award, which is awarded only to those agents with a policy persistency rating of 90 percent or higher. Moreover, more than 60 percent of the agents with us for three or more years achieved the designation of Chartered Life Underwriter (CLU). The CLU designation is conferred by The American College and requires candidates to pass a series of examinations on a variety of financial planning topics as well as satisfying character and experience requirements.

Those statistics were all great measures of our success. But there are other measures that I value as much, if not more.

Nominally my job was in life insurance sales—after all I managed a life insurance agency. But, whereas I once achieved a lot of success in sales, it had been a long time since that was my focus. Ever since I became a district agent in 1966, my primary focus has been that of building relationships upon which our firm and its success could stand. I've tried everything. I've read hundreds (no exaggeration) of management books. I've hired psychotherapists to help our associates with business and personal problems. I've even hired handwriting specialists to help in our selection process, as well as to assist us in developing the best training for our associates. The folks in Northwestern's corporate office in Milwaukee found my methods questionable—to put it politely. However, when I began to succeed their attitude became, "Oh well as long as he produces he can do it his way." Before long they were coming to me for advice and asking me to help them to develop training modules and to speak to other General Agents. And I gladly helped in any way I could.

In my years at the agency, I did my very best to find ways to have our representatives feel supported so that they could do their jobs and be productive and personally successful

I've also attempted to figure out what parts of my job were most rewarding to me and how I could best use my resources to help our associates succeed. A large part of what I developed came from what I observed when I was in sales. I particularly noted how salespeople were treated by some managers—treatment that was not only wrong and unfair but also was counter-productive. A lot of "my stuff" came about as a result of trial and error. Things that I tried that flatly failed. The manner in which I did or didn't delegate work, the net result usually being that I had too much to do and problems didn't get solved. I could go on and on.

From my experiences and observations I developed what I call "The 22 Principles," It is no exaggeration to say that our agency's success rests on these tenets of management. In fact, I'll go even further than that and say that we can measure success by how well we adhere to these principles.

I have been conducting seminars for district managers, new general agency managers, and experienced general agency managers for many years. During theses seminars I teach and demonstrate the principle you will find in this book. People keep listening and coming back to hear my message year after year, so they must be deriving some benefit from what I bring to them.

What I ultimately want you to know about managing is that the true end result of practicing and relying on the 24 Principles can be fun. Yes Fun!! My job was fun. I can get into my car and drive anywhere within our agency's territory and see my associates with happy families, leading good lives. It makes me proud. They own their homes and have money in the bank. They have neat kids and are involved with their families. They're involved in their communities and with each other. They lead balanced lives. It's enjoyable to be with people for whom life has worked out so well.

You can build a successful operation and not have such a good time; not have the relationships you would like to have; not make the money you would like to make. The goal of the 22 Principles is to assist you in building your organization so that you can have a balanced life; terrific, rewarding relationships; and earn the money you want to earn.

I firmly believe that by looking to the 24 Principles for guidance you too can achieve the success you desire and have fun in the process. You can experience the joy of management.

TAKING THE HIGH ROAD TO THE BOTTOM LINE

PRINCIPLE 1
The Salesperson Is My Client

This chapter introduces my most fundamental and most revolutionary concept. A concept that turns the popularly accepted corporate pyramid upside down and stands ii on its head. A concept that the corporate environment has an enormous problem accepting. I maintain that "My sales representative is my client" is the watchword by which all of a manager's actions must be judged.

In our system management has a responsibility to do all in its power to help the sales force do its job properly and successfully. That may mean getting involved at a level beyond the traditional business relationship. It may mean being continuously available to provide advice. It may mean being involved with an associate's family, celebrating births, marking family milestones, attending funerals, and so on. These personal touches are essential to building a strong and enduring relationship between the manager and the sales associate.

This first of the 22 Principles is the single most important of all. It forms the basis for everything we do.

Let's take a look at this concept. How, ideally, would you treat a valued client? Any salesperson (in this instance you) worth his or her salt is going to treat a client with respect. You are going to provide the client with whatever he or she might need to the best of your ability. This might mean going out of your way to educate the client about the products and services you offer. It might mean keeping track of the client's situation over an extended period of time to be sure that his or her needs continue to be met. It might mean helping the client to determine whether he or she can benefit from another product or service you provide. If the client has difficulty understanding what you are talking about, you will patiently explain it again, assuming the client is serious enough to warrant that attention. You will also show respect for that client on a personal level. You learn the names of family members and inquire as to their well-being. You send a greeting card or perhaps a gift at birthdays or holidays. If there is death in the family you convey your sympathy and perhaps attend the funeral services.

Why do you do these things? Why all this attention? You are expressing your gratitude to the client for bringing his or her business your way. You are honoring the client for coming to you when he or she could just as easily have found similar products or services elsewhere.

The most important thing for any business owner or sales manager to recognize is that your salespeople are bringing **THEIR** business to you. They are the ones who are out there every day selling and winning clients for your company. They are the people creating the revenue that keeps your company afloat and makes it successful. They are the reason you have a job. Your salespeople are your clients and you must keep this in mind in your every interaction with them. Just as any good salesperson works for his or her client, you should, and must, work for your salespeople. You have to attend to their business and personal needs as diligently as you would for a valued client.

PRINCIPLE 1

For most managers this is a concept that is difficult to grasp and, at first, even more difficult to practice. Especially for those who are new to management. Far too often new managers think that their new position means that they are important. But the reality is very different. The reality is that the sales representatives, normally, don't want a new manger. They don't readily welcome the newcomer. They prefer that which they have to the unknown new arrival. They, like most of us, are resistant to change. The fact is that the new manager has to prove himself or herself to the people he or she is to manage. The reality is that the new manager is not a "big deal" to the sales force until he or she has proven themselves. In my seminars for new managers I always advise them to conduct an in-depth fact-finding interview with each and every salesperson. During these interviews they should "listen, not talk!" I urge them to ask how they can be of service to their sales people. I strongly recommend that they don't walk in and immediately set down new rules and regulations. I remind them that they have to earn the respect of their salespeople and that their success depends on how well they help the sales representatives do their jobs

PRINCIPLE 2
Facilitate Responsibility

"Facilitate responsibility" is, surprisingly, the advantageous flip side of recognizing the sales representative as your client. When new salespeople are put into the crucible of a new and demanding job, they will look to put the blame for failures and disappointments on someone else, namely management. If, however, management is doing everything possible to help them succeed, those same people will put the responsibility where it belongs, on themselves. And they will make the adjustments they must make if they are to be successful.

In discussing this principle the points I will cover are:

(a) the goal of having the sales representatives take responsibility for their own successes and failures
(b) why salespeople who are struggling look for someone to blame
(c) how making the sales representative your client forces her or him to become more responsible.

To do their jobs effectively sales representatives need more than just product knowledge and awareness of the mechanics of a sale. They also need accountability for their actions. If a salesperson is going to receive accolades, pats on the back, and commissions for one's successes, that same person must be willing to acknowledge that the responsibility for failures is also his or hers. Without this accountability for failures, a sales representative cannot and will not grow in the job or learn what needs to be learned. He or she will just keep doing the same things over and over with the same results.

Some managers, when they think about treating the salesperson as a client, think that it must involve a lot of coddling—a lot of doing for the representatives what they should be doing for themselves. In fact it is just the opposite. In reality making the salesperson the client forces that person to take full responsibility for all of his or her actions, whether they lead to success or failure.

Every salesperson faced with a failure is going to look for someone to blame. The more talented the representative, the greater the chance he or she will try to shift blame, because they are not accustomed to failing. And take a guess who is most often in the line of fire: management. How many times have we in management heard, "They never told me," or "You didn't," or "I didn't get the support," or any one of hundreds more. At our agency we have always had a goal, an insidious goal. The goal is to give our sales force no excuses whatsoever. It is a diabolical plan. We strive to provide them with so much assistance that no one can say, "I'm not getting enough help." I am constantly asking my associates, "Are you getting all the support you need?" "Is there anything we can do to help you?" It is also why I continually encourage them to take advantage of the people in our offices who can be a resource for them. The whole purpose is to remove the opportunity for them to lay off blame, to blame someone else. They have to look at themselves and only at themselves. The only way for any of us to succeed is to look at ourselves. Your goal should be to make your performance as manager so airtight that your representatives are forced to put the blame for failing on themselves. And, to take the steps they need to take to remedy their shortcomings. Making the sales representative the client forces the salesperson to put the blame where it belongs: on himself or herself. If you have done everything you could possibly have done to help that associate succeed there is nothing he or she can blame you for. Only if a salesperson takes ownership in his or her part in a failure will he or she take responsibility for not making that same mistake again. In an organization this continued emphasis on owning your mistakes and learning from them creates a culture of self improvement. It creates an atmosphere where people continue to grow in their jobs. And, when they grow, your business grows right along with them.

PRINCIPLE 3
Be Present

What does it mean to "be present?" It means making the person you are: with feel like the most important person in your life at that moment. It means trying your hardest to understand that person and doing your best to reflect back to them that which they need. Being present begins the minute your associate walks into your office for a meeting. It starts with the first handshake when you look directly into his or her eyes and not over a shoulder.

The points I will cover are:

(a) hints for being present
(b) focusing your mind
(c) wrist watch pitfalls
(d) listening
(e) giving thoughts and advice
(f) not being judgmental
(g) the hows, and, more importantly, the whys of being present.

Being present is an essential skill in the sales process. My managers and I teach it to every salesperson in our firm using the methods outlined in this section. And I vigorously maintain it is an equally necessary skill for managing salespeople. It is essential to making the sales representative feel like your client, and essential to helping employees realize that you have their best interests in mind.

When you are "present" you allow the person you are with to feel like the most important person in your life at that moment—which he or she should be. Your mind is not wandering. You are not thinking about your next meeting. You are 100 percent with that person so that when the meeting is over, he or she knows that you have sincerely tried to understand them. This is a real challenge because none of us believes that anyone ever understands us.

What does being present do for your associates? It assures them that you have their best interests at heart. Furthermore, it assures them that you will do your very best to help them. In addition, if you are "present," it makes it easier for them to accept criticism. A coaching consultant who worked with our agency sales force for almost 30 yearst used to say to me, "Phil, I can never understand how you get away with saying the things you say to your people." I can be tough. Over the years I have said some really, really tough things to my associates. What amazed this consultant was that after I was so tough on them, they would come and thank me. And, they would tell others in almost a bragging way, what I said to them. I know why this occurred. It's because I was so present and attentive they knew that I said what they needed to hear in order to succeed.

One of the most important things in "being present" is knowing how to listen. In order to be a good listener you must have your mind clear. Before any meeting whether it's with a sales prospect, a new recruit, your best salesperson, or one of your management people, you must focus your mind. Think about who you will be meeting with, what might he or she want or need from you, and what can you do for that person. Clear your mind of everything else. Before an important meeting I will not allow my staff to present me with problems. Nor will I read any correspondence. I will do nothing that might cause me to take my eye off the ball during the meeting. I am an easily distracted person so being present is a challenge for me. Therefore I set things up in ways to help myself. I don't wear a wristwatch because I don't want to risk that distraction. I think it is demeaning if you check your watch during a meeting. I will not take phone calls during a meeting, not even from my family. The only exception is in the event of an emergency. Also, I never sit at my desk during a meeting. There could be papers or publications on my desk which might attract my attention. And, I always sit with my back to the door. In our offices people would often open my door and peek in. If they saw my back, they knew not to interrupt and to come back at another time. These quirks of habit may sound strange but they point out how important "being present" is to me.

After ensuring that you have and can maintain a clear head comes the next key aspect of listening, that is, don't butt in. Allow a person to talk through that which is on his or her mind. Pay them the courtesy of honoring their perspective by letting them tell their story without interruption. Then, repeat back that which was said in your own words. This will help confirm that you heard correctly and conveys to the other party that you want to understand. During this feedback affirm that which you believe he or she did well. You must also offer input on that which could have been done differently or better. Always explain the ways in which you suggestions may be beneficial.

An effective manager must also strive to be non-judgmental. Not being judgmental is another aspect of "being present." If you are judgmental it causes the other person to feel that he or she has less worth in your eyes. Being judgmental often comes across as insulting and demeaning. Very few people can be insulted into changing or improving. That person will most likely tune you out, shut you off, and stop hearing what you are saying. He or she will become defensive and close up. On the other hand if you make that person feel worthwhile, and convey that you are helping them improve on the valuable person they already are, they will listen attentively. If you don't damage an ego, humiliate, or devalue someone, he or she will be receptive to your advice and suggestions.

Being present is one more way we help our clients, the sales people, be the best they can be.

PRINCIPLE 4
Be Gracious

"Be gracious" is the principle that I have found brings me the most joy in my job. Being gracious means doing things for others with an open heart. Some managers I have known seemed to believe that if they showed reluctance to doing something for their sales force, whether it be extending a deadline or hosting an office they would be more appreciated when they finally did so. I believe just the opposite. I believe that doing things graciously not only assures that management will be appreciated for their actions, it also gives the manager incredible satisfaction for what he or she has done.

In this section I will cover:

(a) what it means to be gracious
(b) how being gracious breeds a healthy sense of obligation
(c) how it makes your job easier and more fun
(d) expressions that convey graciousness
(e) how to be gracious during an argument.

"Be gracious"—if you master this principle you can truly enjoy managing a sales team. Being gracious sounds simple but far too many managers just are not. Or, perhaps, they don't know how to be gracious. An important thing to note about being gracious is that the perception is more important than the reality. Let me give you an example: I had friend who was viewed as cheap, stingy, greedy, and so on, by his salespeople, his management team, and his staff. He was called all kinds of names behind his back. However, I was privy to his financial information. I was amazed to see that in the area of promotions and incentive, i.e. trips, contests, parties, etc., his figures were, percentage-wise, the same as mine and perhaps even a bit higher. Yet, in our agency, the perception was that I was very generous and not hesitant to spend money, which was also how I thought of myself. The difference between us and the reason he was perceived so differently was that he did everything grudgingly. His demeanor let you know that he did not like doing these things. As a result whenever he gave, he took all the fun out of it. He was the guy who flicked the lights off and on ten minutes early at a party. Or, he sponsored a sales contest that was so tough that very few could win it. The numbers said that he had earned an undeserved reputation, but his attitude said he earned and deserved it. His associates felt his resentment toward sharing the pot.

I learned about graciousness from two very important people in my life. The first was my dad. He was an extraordinarily gracious person and I learned so much by watching how he related to people. I grew up in Brooklyn, N.Y., where my dad owned a drug store on Third Avenue in the Bay Ridge section. Below Third Avenue were very wealthy people, and above Third Avenue were very poor people. Dad treated everyone well but was especially gracious to those who didn't have much. He did whatever he could do to help them. He was known as Dr. Pierz because he was not only their pharmacist, he was also their neighborhood clinic. Those folks would come to him to treat all kind of minor illnesses. Many times he would give them medication when they couldn't afford to go to a doctor. He would probably be sent to jail if he were doing those things today. And, whatever he did was done with graciousness. He was sincerely happy to be of help and he was respected for it. I have always admired that about him and have tried to emulate it.

PRINCIPLE 4

The second person was my general agent, Bill Griffin. As a young agent, I moved from Washington, D.C., to Hartford, Conn. to work with Bill because I'd heard that he was an unusual person and greatly admired.

One of the many things he taught me was, "Never lend anybody money, if you don't want to. And if you do lend money, make the borrower feel good about it. Don't lend it if you can't lend it graciously or you will have lent money and will not be appreciated for having done so. And neither you nor the borrower will feel good about it."

"Oh alright" is not a gracious response to a loan request. Neither is, "I will but you shouldn't have gotten yourself into this bind," nor is "I am not feeling good about this." If you decide to lend money, do so graciously, e.g. "I trust in you and I believe in you. If this will help you I'm happy to do it and I will trust you to do the right thing."

I don't recommend being gracious just because it is a nice thing to do. It is also in your self interest. When you do something graciously you are appreciated for it and you feel personally good about it. Advance money graciously, take joy in the parties you host, the contests you sponsor. If there is any question as to whether or not an associate has won a prize or a contest, give it to him or her. I am not suggesting you give away the shop. But, if there is any doubt, being seen as the hero is far more important than the dollars it will cost.

Being gracious is enjoyable, and is appreciated far beyond the effort it requires. If you are not gracious, you miss a tremendous opportunity to really shine. Being gracious is, however, more than just a way of acting. It is a state of being. I have felt privileged that I have had it in my power to be able to help people when they are down. To host parties that bring such good times. To take a sales representative and his or her family on that trip of a lifetime.

Whatever you do for your salespeople, be gracious about it. If you are gracious you are saying to them, "I hold you in high regard, the highest regard". You are letting then know that they are your valued clients.

How many businesses do you know of that have a family tree? Ours did.

Another measure of our success, in fact a measure of which I am extremely proud, is the number of our representatives who were brought into the agency by people already working there. An agent might recommend a friend or perhaps a client who would join us. Then that new associate might later recommend a friend who might recommend a brother or sister and on and on. This is the way our agency's family tree grew. Why did these associates recruit family and friends? They did so because they loved what they did and where they did it. And, having people around them they were close to made it even better.

Because I was always searching for ways to let my associates know that I valued their input, I would often ask them why they referred others to our agency. The answers I received were consistent and rewarding. I was constantly told that they were comfortable referring people to us because they knew that their referrals would be treated with honesty and dignity. Moreover, they knew that those folks we invited to join us would receive the best training, supervision and support we could possibly provide. As one associate said to me, "Phil, I know you're going to treat him just as well as you treat me."

PRINCIPLE 4

The net result of these agent referrals? Our agency contracted one new sales associate out of every 12 new recruiting interviews. The industry average at that time was one new recruit from every 60 interviews. My clients, the sales representatives, were helping me to be more efficient, more effective, and a lot happier in my job.

PRINCIPLE 5
Respect Your Representative's Efforts to "Grow Up"

The relationship between a sales manager and a sales representative changes over time in much the same way as the relationship between a parent and a child undergoes change. But, whereas the rebellious years of a teenager are certainly a trial for the parents, the parent-child bond generally lasts. All too often a representative's efforts to break away and establish his or her identity on the job nearly end the relationship between manager and salesperson. This section explains this dynamic and deals with how a manager can and should continue to treat the agent as a client.

The points covered are:

(a) the "teenage" years for agents
(b) the "parent-child" syndrome
(c) feeling hurt and withdrawing
(d) preserving and altering the relationship.

Being a parent is a tough job. One of the reasons it is so tough is that it it constantly changing. When your kids are babies they need feeding, diapering, and pampering. When they get a bit older they need to be allowed to roam and explore at the same time they are being protected. And, when they reach the teenage years, about the time they start to take responsibility, they begin questioning everything you say and do. They question your values, your methods, your authority, In general they give you a hard time.

Nevertheless, you have to find the resources within you to still love them and support them. Unfortunately, sales managers have to go through this process not only with their children but with their agents as well. And, unfortunately, while most parents make a real effort to stick it out emotionally during those difficult teen years, in the reasonable expectation that a well-rounded person will reemerge, many sales managers distance themselves from their teenage representatives. In many instances, the relationship can never be repaired.

Relationships with kids and sales representatives run the same course. When agents are new they look at you with respect and admiration. You know how to do the job and they don't. Career-wise they are almost totally dependent on you. For the manager it's a bit of an ego trip to get this kind of respect and to have people willing to follow everything you say. However, three to five years down the road this changes. If things are going well, the way you actually want them to be going, each of these "kids" will have become quite self-sufficient and may be feeling a little cocky about his or her abilities. Then he or she attends a sales school or a sales conference that you sent them to. Upon their return you learn that your profit-sharing system is no longer to their liking. Nor are your sales requirements. Or, your attendance rules. And, you are told this by this person who once hung on your every word. The problem is that too many managers take these criticisms personally. You've brought up these people, taught them everything they know, taken their phone calls at 11 p.m. at night, and this is how they repay you? Sadly, most managers react by withdrawing from these "teenagers." However, when you withdraw from them you are no longer making them your clients. And, you are no longer working toward the goal you both share, namely, to have them and your business succeed and grow.

PRINCIPLE 5

What must you, the manager, do to forge an altered and lasting relationship with these maturing salespeople? You must not take this "maturing" process personally. You must continue to build on the "valued client" relationship. You must continue to see and recognize their talent despite the current difficulties. You must exercize patience with their need to challenge you. It is your job to help them understand that you respect their desire to think and work independently, but that we all have frameworks within which we must operate. Explain your rules and their purposes. Be sure they understand your reasons for establishing sales requirements and attendance. Outline you thought process in setting up the profit-sharing system or whatever is being challenged. Convey your sincere desire to find new ways to help them as they continue to grow. Above all be open and non-defensive.

As with raising teenagers, these years are not easy. But with enough love and patience you and your representatives will get through them. Hang in with them as you would with a good client. Ultimately it is exciting to see them maturing through these changes as they learn to respect the company's, as well as your, boundaries and requirements. If handled properly this maturing process can lead to a different but more meaningful relationship. And, it can be a joy for you to be a part of it.

As you can see these principles piggy back upon each other. The transition through the "growing up" phase will be considerably less difficult if you did "facilitate the agent's taking responsibility." If you have been "present" during the intervening years the trust level established will help both of you during these trying times.

PRINCIPLE 6
Don't Neglect Your Best

The manager-salesperson relationship reaches yet another stage when the student surpasses the teacher. That is, when the representative becomes better at the sales process than the manager had ever been. At this point another break in the relationship may occur because the manager may feel he has nothing to offer this veteran agent. He may believe that his time is better spent supporting struggling representatives. This can be a costly mistake. I learned this lesson when one of my best agents threatened to leave me. I learned that no matter how successful agents become they need their sales manager to be there for them.

In this section I will discuss:

(a) interacting with agents who move beyond you
(b) the temptation to retreat
(c) these are your best "clients"
(d) what these high achievers want more than anything.

I learned principle number six the hard way—I darned near lost my best salesman and a very good friend. As managers we know that a major part of our job is to bring new salespeople into the business. To nurture them and train them. To give them the benefit of our knowledge and experience. To show them how to be successful and to enjoy what they do. It's exciting and gratifying when you have someone finally get the hang of the job and get to selling successfully. But what happens after they've "gotten it?" When you don't think there is anything more you could conceivably teach them? They no longer need you, right? Wrong!!

I had an associate like this. Let's call him George. He had been an agent with us for about ten years and had far surpassed any of the milestones I had achieved when I was out in the field selling. I considered George to be one of my closest friends. We went to lunch one day, as we occasionally did, and I expected our usual comfortable conversation about work, family, sports, or the newspaper headlines. Wow, was I wrong!

George started our lunch meeting by complaining about the sales builder (a sales/personal growth) group he was in. Then he muttered about the fact that he had to hire his own secretary. He lashed out at me about several other things and finished by saying, "By the way you owe me $32,000." I was crushed. Why in the world was he attacking me? I thought he should be thanking me. I believed I deserved credit for helping him accomplish his goals. It was all I could do not to tell him, "Fine leave the agency" and to storm out of the restaurant. Fortunately, because we were close friends and had a history together we kept talking. We had a round of drinks. And, then at last he said, "Phil, that was all garbage. The real issue is you don't pay attention to me anymore." Needless to say I was floored. Do you know why I wasn't paying as much attention to him? It was because I didn't know what I could do for him. He had so far surpassed anything I had ever done in sales. I didn't think he needed me any longer. That wasn't so. He wanted a continuation of our relationship. He needed to know that my moral support was still there and that he was still my "client."

PRINCIPLE 6

That incident changed my life as a general agent and as a sales manager. From that time on, no matter how large our agency grew, I was always involved in the sales builder groups for our big producers. I stayed close with all those people who were so much better at sales than I ever was and they loved it. They wanted me with them not because of my knowledge of new products or new sales techniques. In fact, at times, I hardly knew what they were talking about. Nevertheless, I could still advise them on their relationships with clients; or, perhaps, or how best to approach a particular prospective client. But what was most valuable to them was that I continued to be there—for them and with them.

A successful manager has to be there for his top producers as well as for those who are just learning the business. Your top producers need you to be there offering your talents and strengths when needed. They need to know that you are following their progress and taking an on-going interest in them so that they can feel cared about and important to you.

Here are some of the things you can do to convey that message to them:

(1) attend their sales meetings
(2) stay apprised of their progress
(3) give freely of your admiration for their accomplishments
(4) make a point of meeting face-to-face every few months, perhaps for breakfast or lunch or a cocktail, so that they feel your presence in their lives
(5) ask about their families and be sure to follow up later with relevant questions, congratulations, or condolences.

These associates are, after all, your best "clients." If they want your time you must be sure to be available to them. The top producers don't ask for much time. They, like you, are also very busy. But they need to know you are there.

PRINCIPLE 7
Make "Helping Others" Part of Your Culture

"Help others" is an agency wide tenet in our system. It is a rock-solid foundation for the way we conduct our day-to-day business. Assisting newer representatives is not just a favor that the veterans bestow, it is an obligation. No one receives any additional compensation for providing this assistance, yet the system works. It is all part of making the salesperson the client. My management team and I make certain that we regularly have conversations with every new agent during which we ask, "Are you getting all the help you need?" If the answer is not an unequivocal yes we will personally find someone to assist with whatever is needed. If the answer is yes, we solicit from that new associate a promise to help those who come after them. I have no doubt that this makes all the difference in the culture of a workplace. And, in the feelings of the sales representatives about their jobs.

In this section I will discuss:

(a) the phenomenon of reciprocity among agents
(b) why helping others is not just a nice thing to do
(c) a culture of helping requires that everyone gets all the help needed
(d) a helping culture creates an open door, trusting environment
(e) territorial disputes must be dealt with properly or they can destroy your culture.

Ed Koch, the former mayor of New York, once said, "Make your environment so good that you can only blame yourself at the end of the day." I have always done my best to have this be so our agency.

Some people have derisively called The Pierz Agency a love fest. Well, I'm proud to tell you that it was a trusting, caring place. The salespeople trusted and helped each other. No one locked their door. If not a love fest, it was certainly a trust fest. This kind of environment, where representatives can be nurtured and helped to thrive, does not come through luck. It takes a lot of hard work and strong beliefs.

New additions to our sales team first heard about the "helping others" principle at the very end of our initial training session. I would tell them, "Now that you are here you have the right to go to any other associate and ask for help, and to expect that it will be given to you. It might not necessarily be right that minute but you will be helped. I'm going to repeatedly ask you, as we progress through these next weeks, if you are indeed getting all the help you need. And, if you are not, I will not rest until I find it for you".

The happy news is that, almost without exception, the answer would be "Yes" and I would ask, "Are you sure now?" "Yes." In the rare instance when the answer was "No," I'd stop whatever I was doing and take that person directly to his or her immediate supervisor and say, "This new associate needs help, what are we going to do to provide it?"

As a part of this process I would always explain that this right to get help from other representatives came at a price. That it carried with it an obligation: that when they got far enough along in their careers, they would be available to give support to a new member of the sales team.

PRINCIPLE 7

Hardly a day went by without one salesperson telling me about something nice done by another associate. I would be told about someone who had gone out of his or her way to be of help. Our experienced salespeople would take the time to explain products, or to drill a new associate on sale techniques. At times they would go on sales calls with someone new and give that new agent feedback and constructive criticism. They would even meet with a new representative's spouse and talk about the necessity for the long and late hours beginning this career. They didn't do these things because it was part of the job; and they were not paid for their efforts. They did these things because, in prior years, veterans had helped them when they were new and in that same boat. They were carrying on the tradition of helping, and, in doing so, they were strengthening our culture. You can be sure that I made these veterans aware of how much their help was appreciated.

This spirit of helping was not limited to the experienced agents helping the newbies. Our veterans continuously consulted with, and helped, each other, They got to know each other's strengths and became referral sources for each other. They called each other in to work jointly on cases. These things happened because they had invested in their fellow agent and therefore wanted him or her to succeed. It was not "You win, I lose," it was "We both win"

The environment of mutual trust, of helping and obligation that we fostered had many benefits. The first was that our new representatives' learning curves climbed dramatically because they had mentors constantly available to them. And, when their learning curve went up, so did their earning curve because they quickly became more knowledgeable about products and more skilled in making sales presentations. Another benefit was that our office became a place where agents felt loved and supported. The other salespeople were their friends and supporters, not their competitors. Certainly they had their differences, but they were minimized because they all had a common investment in each other. They had a desire to see each other win and succeed. When our representatives left the office to go on sales calls, they left feeling liked, and likeable, which helped boost them in their meetings with clients.

There was one very important element to making this culture work; his name is Joe Kardas. Joe was a member of our management team, a sales trainer, and our resident computer expert. More importantly, he also had the responsibility for mediating any and all territorial disputes. I learned a long time ago that these disputes cannot be allowed to sit and fester. They must be resolved as quickly as possible so that everyone can move on. I also discovered that it was best if the resolution of the dispute was not my decision. Therefore, Joe had the final word in these matters. He could not be overruled, even by me. Joe was very fair, very tough, and highly respected. Once he made his decision his word was law. And, everyone then got back to work—and back to helping each other.

PRINCIPLE 8
Make your Producers your Recruiters

For any sales operation, recruitment is it's lifeline. Without a steady supply of qualified new talent, a sales business cannot grow. Many managers spend an inordinate amount of time seeking out, interviewing, and bringing new recruits on board. Even in the most successful sales organizations, recruiters see an average of 60 or more prospective agents for every one they hire. Needless to say, this is a costly and time-consuming process. Recruiting is necessary but it doesn't have to be a dreaded chore.

In our agency one out of every 12 prospective agents who we interviewed joined us. Moreover, our agency retained slightly more than 30 percent of its hires after four years; compared to less than 15 percent industry wide. Why were our recruiting efforts so successful? The answer lies in the fact that our producers were our recruiters.

When your associates are happy in their jobs, when they know they are your clients, they seek out interested and qualified friends and family members to bring into the fold. They become a powerful tool in your recruiting arsenal. In turn, these friends and family members are motivated to join, not only because of management's efforts and promises but also due to the positive recommendation of someone they know and trust.

In this section, the points I will discuss are:

(a) the advantages of making your producers your recruiters
(b) why new recruits brought in by active producers have the best chance of succeeding
(c) the savings in time and money
(d) the advantage of having an office full of "begots,"

So, how did we find these golden people? What made what we had to offer so much more appealing to them than other opportunities? The answer to the first question is that our existing representatives found these people for us. The best way to get agents is through agents. They know what the job requires and they know intuitively if someone will be good at it. The answer to the second question is that our producers sold the career for us.

Our agency was truly an agency of "begots," a term I took from the Bible. There is a section of the Bible about progeny: "And Arpachshad begot Shelah; and Shelah begot Eber; and unto Eber were born two sons......." Well our agency was not unlike that. Bob Derrenbacher recruited George Turner; and George brought in Mike McKeever who in turn recruited Bob McCann; and so on; and so on. Virtually every one of our producers brought a friend or family member onto the team. One of our agency publications, titled, "Quest for Quality," featured two full pages showing the charts of "begots." It was an impressive thing to see. The vast majority of our agents were referred to us by our agents. They brought in a sibling or a cousin or a friend or client. Why did they bring these people they knew and loved to us? Because they knew we would treat them as valued clients.

The Northwestern conducted an Agents Attitude Survey every two years. Our agency consistently came out ahead of

PRINCIPLE 8

company average. In 1998, the last time this particular question was asked, 100 percent of our agents said they felt comfortable referring others to join our agency. This contrasted to 60 percent companywide. What was our secret? Why were our representatives so confident about recommending our agency to others? It was because we made our representatives our clients. They could tell prospective agents, with confidence, that, if they were to join our agency, they would be well trained and well supervised in a happy, productive environment. The prospective new hire came to us with an inclination to trust us because a relative or friend said we could be trusted. The wariness, skepticism, and tension normal in that situation were dramatically reduced leading to a much more productive meeting. A manager cannot buy the kind of trust and loyalty it takes for an associate to refer a friend or loved one to the business. This type of trust and loyalty must be earned. This kind of trust and loyalty comes about when the producer knows that he or she is your client

The benefits of recruiting in this manner are invaluable. There are numerous advantages to treating your representatives as your clients so that they will help you in your recruiting efforts. When you have an office full of "begots" you have people who already know each other; they have a built-in connection. And, the new representatives have ready, willing, and able mentors. These things go a long way in helping to build a supportive environment where everyone is on the same team. The culture you've worked to create is endorsed and enhanced. Recruiting costs, in time spent and in money spent, are greatly reduced. And, most important, the vital task of recruiting become much easier and a lot more fun.

PRINCIPLE 9
Be Honest with Potential Recruits

At our agency we took a different and unique approach, after the initial contact, with a potential recruit. The hallmark of this approach—HONESTY! I taught our recruiters to begin not by selling the career, but by telling the candidates why people fail at sales. This helped the weaker candidates to weed themselves out, thereby reducing future turnover. Our recruiters gave each candidate a list of current sales representatives names, and we urged the candidates to call these representatives and ask whatever they wanted to ask. We did not inform the representatives that we had done so. This gave the candidate a true picture of what the job entailed, and it also helped us to judge a candidates initiative. In this section I'll cover:

(1) being honest and straightforward during the recruiting process
(2) telling potential sales associates, at the onset, what makes the job tough and why people fail at it
(3) urging candidates to speak with current agents without restrictions
(4) making spouses an integral part of the recruiting process.

Honesty = The Best Policy

Our agency took an approach to dealing with prospective representatives that was very different from most commission-based sales organizations. The norm is to try to sell the ndidates on the job. We, on the other hand, tried to scare them away. This approach was a key element in attempting to sort out the people who couldn't make in our business from those who could succeed.

In the first interview we did point out some of the advantages of the career, e.g. being your own boss, setting your own hours, eventually earning a sizable income. But we also tried very hard to shock people by telling them everything we could about what was wrong with our business. The starting point was a discussion about the stigma attached to the title "Life Insurance Salesperson." We talked about cold calling on the telephone; the long and late hours in the early years; and, most assuredly, the constant rejection.

If we hadn't scared off the candidate by this time we went on and discussed the most common pitfalls for a new associate. We talked about the inability to cope with rejection; the financial strain when getting started; the refusal to adhere to training; the disaster of disorganization; and the peril of a negative attitude. We asked the candidate whether he or she suffered from any of these tendencies and, if so, might that compromise his or her ability to succeed in our business.

The people we were searching for, those who were success-oriented, would have a very different reaction to this information than the average interviewee. The success-oriented would reject the idea that he or she might have these problems. That person might say, "I don't even hear the word no." Or," I understand that you people are the experts here and I want to learn everything you can teach me about how to succeed in this business." At this point the direction of the interview would start to shift, instead of us telling them about our career opportunity they began selling themselves to us. If we got a good feeling about a candidate during this

PRINCIPLE 9

interview we would move him or her further in the requ process.

"Testing 1 — 2 — 3 Testing"

The next step in our process was to administer several tests to a candidate to try to determine if the candidate was meant for our business. We used these tests to help us assess whether this person would be able to sell to the public, whether he or she was a team player, and whether he or she could tolerate rejection. We used these tests religiously but we never ignored our personal reactions to, and our assessments of a candidate. That is to say, we also always listened to our "gut."

Upon receiving the test results, we would set up an interview to review them with the candidate. We carried out this step in the process even if we had decided not to go any further with that candidate. Why? Because we owed the candidate that courtesy and it was the "honest" thing to do.

Another important part of our recruitment process was to encourage the prospective agents to talk to our current agents. We would provide the candidate the names of ten to 15 of our salespeople and encourage the candidate to call them and ask anything about the agency or the career or whatever. We didn't alert these folks that we had given out their names, and we certainly did not brief them or rehearse them on what to say. We wanted them to respond as spontaneously and as honestly as possible. We wanted them to feel free to say whatever they wished to say.

The primary objective was to give the candidate a true picture of what the job entailed (87.5 percent of our agents told a company sponsored survey that, "new recruits are given a realistic picture of the agent's job," as compared to 47.7

percent throughout the Northwestern network). A secondary objective was to test the candidate's initiative; how willing was a candidate to pick up the phone and call a stranger? And, would that candidate be too intimated to do so. We then would ask our agents what they thought of the candidate, and we took their opinions very seriously. (An aside: later, during our training sessions, we asked the recruits how they felt after talking to our agents. We would say, "I'll bet you came away from that conversation feeling good and really liking the place. Why? Because they made you feel important. They are experts at communicating and made you feel that they were really interested in you—which they were. That is what you are about to learn. There is a technique to making people feel this way so that you can earn their trust.")

The point of all this testing was to cull those who could make it in our business from those who couldn't. We were acutely aware of how detrimental to morale it was to have lots of people coming and then going right back out the door. A high turnover rate was not good for anyone, We strove to make reasonably sure that, when we invited a candidate to join us, we had a keeper.

Spouses Are My Clients Also

As part of the final steps in the recruitment process we brought in the recruit's husband, wife, or partner. Our business, initially, involves nights and long hours and that can be hard on a family. We brought the spouse in to meet the firm's principals so that they felt part of things and not left out of the loop. We encouraged them to talk with the spouses of our salespeople. We stated upfront that they could not dictate what hours the new associate could or could not work. These sessions helped us to gauge to what extent the spouse would be supportive of the new recruit. We knew if the spouse was

PRINCIPLE 9

not supportive, either the agent or the marriage would fail. We did not want our business to undermine a family; nor did we want a lack of family support to undermine a recruit's chance for success.

It is important to note that this interview did not end our involvement with the spouses of our salespeople. We did our best to involve the spouses in everything we did. We included the families of our salespeople whenever possible. Our Christmas party and any other office parties included spouses and children. They were family affairs. We hosted an annual dinner-dance for the representatives and their spouses or significant others. And, the prize for practically every sales contest, e.g. a vacation trip, included spouses.

When we felt sure that a candidate was a good fit for our business, we invited him or her into training class. They were now a part of us.

PRINCIPLE 10
Be Involved in Basic Training

You are never too important for training. Training is, and always has been, one of my primary interests and specialties. New sales people throughout the Northwestern network have watched videotapes of my training sessions long after they were recorded, including vintage videos showing me wearing 70s style wide ties and bushy sideburns. And, this continues today long after my retirement as a Northwestern general agent. In this section I'll discuss my strong belief that the top boss—whether that is the general manager of an insurance agency or the CEO of a small company—should always be involved in initial training. The points I will cover are:

(a) the mistake most managers make by removing themselves from basic training
(b) is training a waste of your time or the best time you can spend
(c) the message your involvement sends and the value of it
(d) the typical excuse: "I have to recruit"
(e) the bonding that takes place during initial training.

I make very few exceptions when I say that the top person in just about every company, small, large, or in between, should always be involved in training new associates. Too many managers, as they move up the management ladder, are removed, or remove themselves, from basic training. This operates on the theory that they should only be spending time with the more experienced sales representatives.

Initial training is thought to be a waste of their time, a task better delegated to lower level managers. I contend that just the opposite is true. I believe that not only is it not a waste of time, but, in fact, it is the best time a manager can spend. Moreover, I believe it is extremely valuable time for the trainee and for the manager. Time that pays for itself in many, many ways far into the future. Why? Because the message you send when you take part in training right from the beginning is that you are involved and that you care about them and their learning curve. Furthermore, your involvement tells the recruits that they are important to you and to your organization. Important enough for you to spend many hours with them as they embark on new careers.

Bonding by Being There

Any number of books on child rearing point out that the initial bonding period with babies is the most important. New representatives are like babies in that they are scared. They are nervous. Their antennae are up. They may even be cynical and skeptical. It is a crucial time as far as their faith in your organization is concerned. When you are present for and play a key role in their training, you are beginning the process of bonding with them. A bond that will grow and strengthen for many years into the future. A bond that builds their trust in you and what you say.

In my 31 years as a Northwestern general agent I never missed out on training our new recruits. I was there every day of the five-day initial training course and spent at least three hours with them each day. I personally schooled them in the major training topics of: prospecting for leads, the use of the telephone, fact finding, preparing a sales presentation, and the presentation itself. However, what I did was far less important than the fact that I did it!!

PRINCIPLE 10

When I recommend that they be involved in basic training many managers protest that they are too busy. A typical excuse will be, "But Phil I have to recruit." I am aware that recruiting is a primary responsibility of a sales manager. However, recruiting is more than just bringing in a number of people. It is holding on to those people after you've brought them in. It is giving them a strong foundation for success in your business. I believe a manager owes this to the new recruits and to the organization itself. When you train the new people, when you get involved, you will find that their commitment to your organization begins right at the beginning. You will also find that you don't have to recruit as much because your associates are more likely to stay and succeed and be productive.

Principle 8 Revisited

In Principle 8, I discussed "Making Your Producers Your Recruiters." The point was made that when your producers are happy and secure in their careers, they will help you recruit. If they are successful and productive they will gladly give back to the organization in many ways. And, referring potential salespeople to you will be one of those ways. If you have bonded with them and have gained their trust they might refer a friend or relative to you. The bonding and trust building begins at the beginning and continues to grow during initial training. That bonding and trust building can help create a whole new generation of "begots."

Teach From Where You Were—Not From Where You Are

Hopefully I've convinced you of the importance of a manager being involved in basic training. Now, I'd like to share with you my thoughts about that training.

It's difficult for a manager to remember the days when he or she was young and inexperienced and less than effective. In fact, those are the things an experienced salesperson wants to forget. But, for training purposes, it is essential that a manager remember. I contend that sales managers must remember the mistakes they made when they began selling, and that they should teach and answer questions with those thoughts in mind. This approach to training increases the ability of a new representative to move quickly into effective selling. And, it further strengthens the bond between the manager and the sales force.

Teach the Basics

When it comes to teaching, Vince Lombardi had it right. At the beginning of season, or after a particularly bad performance by the team, he'd begin, "Gentlemen, this is a football." He knew that to be effective a teacher has to start at the basics. For a sales manager this means teaching from where you were—not from where you are.

Experienced, successful salespeople have learned a lot in their careers. And, either because they are justifiably proud and want to show off a little, or because they have forgotten what it's like to be the new guy or gal, they tend to teach from where they are. This is not at all helpful to a trainee. Imagine lining two ladders up against a wall. The first ladder has rungs one foot apart with the first rung one foot off the ground. The second ladder also has rungs one foot apart, but the first rung is three feet off the ground. Now imagine two groups, one for each ladder, each trying to climb those ladders. Which team do you think would get up the ladder more quickly? Teaching from where you are often requires a new agent to try to jump higher, at first, than he or she can possibly jump.

PRINCIPLE 10

Some of your new representatives may be able to make that three foot jump. But, if you teach that way you may miss the good salesperson who cannot start that way. The fact that some new agents may be a little slower at learning, or a bit more fearful, or whatever, does not mean that they won't become great salespeople for you. Remember what it was like when you were new. Remember how frightened you were and how much you didn't know. Put yourself in their shoes and you will be much more effective in helping them get up that first rung.

"This Is a Telephone"

I believe you have to teach the basics of selling, such as developing leads, cold calling, so on. I also believe that you should teach only one system, and that you should teach it consistently. For someone who is experienced it's fine to have choice of methods for gaining a client. For beginners, who are likely nervous and unsure, too much choice causes them to be more unsure. New representatives need a script that works. A system or method that they can, and must, adhere to. They need to be taught the best way to sell as a beginner. And, they must be required to sell using that system until they get on their feet and on the path to success. In a way new representatives are like indentured apprentices until they begin to achieve real success. When they get there, they can sell any way they want to, provided that it is honest, ethical, and effective. Until they reach that point they have to sell following a tried and true system. I firmly believe that constant training in the basics, and constant practicing of the basics is the best way to success.

Teach from where you were when you were new to the business, and teach the basics. That is the best thing you can do for your new representatives—your clients.

PRINCIPLE 11
See People as They Can Be

Over the long haul the best sales representatives aren't necessarily those who catch on most quickly. Those who get off to a fast start don't always sustain and persevere. Conversely, those who start slowly don't necessarily continue to lag behind. With proper training and nurturing a job can be learned and mastered.

In my discussion of this principle I'll talk about:

(a) the tendency to judge people too quickly
(b) the fact that people grow at their own pace
(c) who is worth waiting for: qualities to look for
(d) qualities you cannot and must not tolerate.

One of the biggest mistakes people tend to make in any sales-oriented business is to judge others far too quickly. Because of this tendency a lot of good people don't last in the business. They are lost to our organizations and to the business in general. I'm talking specifically about your new sales representatives. Some of them are going to be quite effective right from the start. They are confident, they follow a script easily, they are on their way without a lot of support from management. It is easy to conclude that these are your golden guys and girls; your future top producers. On the other side of the aisle are the new agents who are really awkward, who, out of nervousness, do something silly or stupid or immature. The new trainees who start slowly and do not hit the ground running.

A lot of managers are quick to say, "Who needs them around here." Well, I'm cautioning you not to be too hasty. I'm encouraging you to give some of those folks more of a chance or you might miss having a really fine person in your organization.

Look For What a Person Can Be

It has been my experience that sales managers have to place more weight on those qualities which are not readily imparted in a training program. Qualities such as honesty, sincerity, accountability, and motivation, to name a few. The qualities and character traits that make up a person's value system. The traits that are an integral part of the type of person you want in your organization.

When I look at a new person, I look for a lot more than whether he or she starts selling right away. I look for their true character traits!! I pay attention to whether that person is caring, honest, and sincere. Those are the things that really matter. I also watch to see how they handle failure. Do they try to hide it or to place the blame somewhere else? People who are up front when they "mess up"—quick to acknowledge it and therefore quick to accept advice on what they can do better—have the toughness and the desire to succeed that really matter in the long run.

They Can Learn To Do the Job—They Really Can

People grow at their own pace, therefore managers must be patient, non-judgmental, and encouraging. Some of my best agents were those who, although they "messed up" in the beginning, were sincere about their mistakes. They didn't try to hide or cover up their errors. They wanted to learn how to correct their mistakes. They strove to

PRINCIPLE 11

stop "messing up." They might not have had a stellar beginning, but they had a desire to succeed. They possessed a "toughness" with themselves and a "toughness" within themselves as to what they wanted to accomplish.

It may take some longer than others to get rolling, but for the right people the wait will be well worth it. They will get there. And, when they do, they will begin to stand out because of their values and their fine qualities. This is what I mean when I say, "See people as they can be." Several of my best salespeople would not have lasted in the business if I had not recognized what they could be, I had not tried to see more in them than appeared at first glance.

It Takes Courage

When working with people who are slow to grow, a manager must keep in mind the relationship among three words: courage, discourage, and encourage. We want our representatives to have courage: the courage to make cold calls; the courage to ask for an appointment; the courage to ask for the sale; and, above all, the courage to challenge themselves. Therefore, we must encourage the. We cannot encourage by discouraging. Comments such as, "If you don't get on the phone you're never going to make it," or "Another bad week," or " Why can't you be consistent?" can lead in only one direction—failure.

We have to give our more reluctant new associates the courage they need to get the job done. I would always point out to theses folks top producers in our agency who struggled when getting started. I would tell them that Joe Superstar once had his doubts also. That he too was scared and reluctant and had also "messed up" and gotten off to a slow start. I would then note the fact that Joe had overcome that stuff—that he had thought and fought his way through it. And that they were capable of doing the same. I'd tell them, "I believe in you and your ability." I'd encourage them and tell them that if they believed in themselves they could also overcome. It is true, if you are patient with these people, if you encourage them and refrain from being discouraging, they will show you exactly what they can be. They will become a benefit to your business and to themselves.

One last thing: Just as you should value and encourage the honest and ethical among your new recruits, you should discourage and run like hell from any liars or cheats or corner cutters who have managed to sneak in the door. No matter how productive they are, no matter how much they sell (some will be very productive and effective), you do not want them around. They are poisonous to a business and to a culture. The sooner they are asked to leave, the better. You don't want those kinds of clients, so, you surely don't want those kinds of salespeople representing you.

PRINCIPLE 12
Special Situations Deserve Special Attention

The special situations I wish to discuss are:

(a) helping the "optional" person and
(b) women in the sales arena.

"Optional" vs. "Procedural"

When it comes to getting things done—especially in a multifaceted job such as sales—I believe there are two types of people. The "procedural" person and the "optional" person. A procedural person is one who recognizes what needs to be done and methodically works at a task until is completed. An "optional" person tends to start one task, then another, and then another, until several things are half done but nothing is quite completed. One could argue that the optional person has no place in sales. I, however, believe that optional people, with their high enthusiasm for new ideas and challenges, can make significant contributions to a sales organization. Yet, without proper structure and support from management, these contributions are bound to be lost. A manager must encourage an optional salesperson to get the necessary help to keep him or her organized and on task. Doing so will allow the optional person's other gifts full expression in the real job of sales representatives: Selling.

I am an optional person. I find it extremely difficult to start a task and stay with it to completion. I am too easily distracted by my other "options." Therefore, I can relate to the problems other optionals face. We are the opposite of procedural people. A procedural person can, and does, follow procedures. He or she gets into the office, figures out what needs to be done that day, or that week, or that month, and then gets it done. Moreover, it gets done in the order in which it should be done. Believe me, as relates to sales, procedural people have a much easier time of things.

A career in sales requires an incredible amount of organization. A salesperson will have many clients, all with differing needs. He or she must correspond with suppliers, people upon whom the completion of a sale is dependent. There are phone calls to make and return; appointments to schedule and keep, nighttime appointments, daytime appointments, calendars to keep under control; and on and on. For someone who is not organized, a career in sales can be like that bad nightmare where you arrive at school and learn there is an exam you haven't studied for. Optional people tend to spend their time on whatever just came up, or on whatever is most exciting to them. They are forever reactive and seldom proactive. This is not a personal fault for which they should be penalized; it is just the way they are. They deserve the same opportunity to succeed as is given to the procedural person at the next desk. As an optional person myself, I have a lot of empathy for others like me. This has helped me understand how I can help those of my agents who are optional people.

Sales Isn't Just Organization.

As mentioned earlier, many people have argued that optional people should not be in sales. Indeed, many optional people have failed at sales for reasons solely related to their optionalness. But a career in sales requires a lot more than merely being organized. It requires enthusiasm for other

PRINCIPLE 12

people. It requires an ability to listen and to understand what is important to the client. It requires a sincere desire to help and to be of service. And, most often, optional people are blessed with these abilities. I contend that optional people can succeed in sales, as I did, if they have the right kind of support.

The most important thing for optional people is to know they are optional. That's half the battle. Once they recognize why they are having difficulty completing a task they can begin to compensate for the problem. There are myriad means available for helping people to organize themselves. There are planning systems and PDA programs designed specifically for salespeople. The best way, however, for my money and the method that worked for me was to surround myself with, and to find support from, people whose strengths are the opposite of mine.

As sales managers it is our responsibility to help our optional salespeople to understand why they are having difficulties and what options are available for dealing with those difficulties. Perhaps, unlike the procedurals who started at the same time, the optional person may need to hire a part-time assistant to set up schedules, handle paperwork, and take care of those things an optional person has difficulty focusing on. The extra expense out of pocket may mean it is going to take more time to build the income level. On the other hand, having help in the office will give the optional person more time to exercise his or her strength, namely, being with other people.

Our principal goal is to do everything we can to make the job work for our representatives whether they be optional or procedural.

"Women in Sales"

In sales, and particularly in the financial services industry, saleswomen have made great strides. With the proper support from management, they will continue to do so.

Today, many sales organizations are trying to recruit female sales representatives. However, these organizations then find they have difficulty retaining those saleswomen. Sales organizations have, historically, been a male domain. As a result they have been slow to recognize the special requirements of many saleswomen, e.g. those who are single parents.

Our agency began recruiting women representatives shortly after I moved into management. For several years we led Northwestern Mutual in sales made by female agents. I believe we did a good job of creating an atmosphere and a culture within which women could succeed and, in fact, stand out as top salespeople. In order to support these folks, our management team had to adapt and to learn. We had to develop a system that enables women to succeed while supporting them in any special issues they might face.

A Valuable Asset

Having female sales representatives is an important asset for any sales organization. The days of men being the major breadwinners, and trusting only other men to advise them, are long gone. Today women make up 53 percent of the U.S. workforce; and, they comprise nearly 30 percent of heads of households. Competent, motivated saleswomen can work equally well with men and women as clients.

Several years ago I realized that there was an enormous pool of talented women who, because of out-dated beliefs,

PRINCIPLE 12

were working at jobs far below their capabilities. These talented people were unhappy and frustrated because they were not being given the opportunity to grow and succeed. Our agency began to actively seek qualified females for our sales force. However, having been an all male sales operation up to this point, we soon learned that we had to adapt to the particular needs of women on the road to success. As you know by now, ours was a "warm, fuzzy, bare-your-soul" agency. A great deal of soul searching went on as our sales representatives were growing into the career. As women joined our sales team, we realized that they were much more sensitive, more open, and more vocal, when it came to expressing their feelings. For them, sensitivity was an asset not a liability. Their sensitivity to the way people responded to them enabled them to work much more effectively with prospective clients and to respond to them appropriately. Unlike many men, they didn't treat every client the same. They were able to tailor their presentation to the recipient, and, as a consequence, were much more likely to reach the prospect and make a sale. This sensitivity was, however, a challenge to our male supervisors who were accustomed to speaking only with male representatives. We found that the tough talk that often worked with males was out. Our saleswomen appreciated straight talk, straightforward assessments of how they were doing and what they needed to do. But, the locker room "get out there and do it men" spiel was something they could not and did not respond to.

We found that managing women took a bit more time. Just about everything required longer discussions because of their thoroughness. We also learned that if our saleswomen had concerns they wanted discuss, it was not a good idea to make them wait. They found it difficult to move forward while an issue was outstanding. It was best to resolve issues as soon as possible so that they could get back to selling

We discovered that it took time for our male representatives to become accustomed to having women in their sales builder groups, and, to become accustomed to indirectly competing with women. At times the salesmen would become impatient with the saleswomen during sales-builder meetings. These clashes had to be adroitly mediated to ensure that these meetings were productive for all. Over time these issues resolved themselves and they certainly don't exist today.

We tried a variety of things to help our saleswomen succeed. Allow me to share with you the single best thing we did. The idea came out of a special meeting involving our management team and the eight female agents we had at that time. We met at a location outside of the agency so as to create a different atmosphere. I started the meeting by telling everyone that management was there to listen; that we wanted input as to how we could better help them; and, that we would not be judgmental or defensive. They told us that they felt that our organization treated them well and fairly. They said that they wanted to be treated the same as the guys, that they wanted to participate in the same sales builder groups and have the same goals. However, they did have other issues that might affect their performance, issues they were not comfortable bringing up in the sales builders. For example, the difficulties of balancing the time demands of working against those of being wives and mothers. Out of this open discussion came the idea for a "women's only" group. Not to replace the sales builder meetings, but to supplement them. We decided that these meetings should be run by a woman. Glenda, our office manager, took on that role.

The group began meeting monthly. Over the years it evolved. It became not only a forum for self-expression but also an opportunity to attend structured workshops on issues

PRINCIPLE 12

such as procrastination, goal setting, and developing good work habits. Attendance was never mandatory but all our female agents attended voluntarily. Eventually a credentialed counselor became the group facilitator. The group was run professionally so that it was not just a place for people to air complaints but a place for our saleswomen to build their skills. The group helped these women to grow personally, and as a result their careers flourished. The results spoke for themselves. Our agency had a higher percentage of saleswomen than the average financial services office and a much higher retention ratio.

This special situation called for special attention for a special group of people: our female sales representatives—our clients.

PRINCIPLE 13
Learn What Motivates Each Salesperson and Teach Him or Her How to Use It

It is fair to say I've been a lifetime student of self-actualization and self-improvement. Over the years I've developed a system for promoting personal achievement that I personally use every day. And, I've taught this system to our salespeople. Combining self-awareness with affirmation and visualization, the system never fails those who are truly committed to it because it calls upon the power of the subconscious to help people attain their goals.

This section outlines this concrete method for achievement, and illustrates how a manager can use the method to help a salesperson identify and attain his or her goals. It also addresses the best way of lighting a fire under someone who is not measuring up.

The points I will discuss are:

(a) the importance of goal setting
(b) "towards pleasure" vs. "away from pain"
(c) external vs. internal: understanding your representative's personal psychology
(d) teaching "The Method:" forgive, acknowledge, affirm, visualize.

Success in sales requires a salesperson to be continually striving, continually reaching out, continually putting himself or herself into new, challenging situations. It takes a lot of energy to keep going like that. Energy that can only come from motivation. It is the sales manager's job to help the agents stay motivated. In my many years of management, I have honed a method that I found always works, with virtually all types of people. It is "The Method" that I taught to my salespeople that they could use every day. I would continuously reinforce the steps of the system for them.

Towards or Away From—External or Internal

Let me explain these important concepts. First and foremost we must understand that these personal responses are exactly and only that—responses. There is no right or wrong response. The purpose in knowing a representative's style is only to help you to motivate and to move that person in the direction you both deem desirable.

Let us begin with people who move towards pleasure. I know them well because I am one of them. What excites and motivates me, for example, is the free time and wherewithal to see this beautiful world. Enjoying holidays with family; walking beaches; dining luxuriously; having the free time to read; having the time to see, taste, and experience everything worthwhile really turns me on. People who move towards pleasure can be depicted in those terms.

Our second, and distinctly different, types of people are those who move "away from" pain. For these people, having a substantial bank account and a low mortgage and a feeling of security and safety is of prime importance. This feeling of safety allows them to "move away" from anxiety and worry. Monies available for their children's education and a secure retirement are strong motivations for this type of person to work hard and succeed.

PRINCIPLE 13

External and internal are terms describing how people experience success. A "towards pleasure" person may be either external or internal. The same is true for an "away from" person. External people need recognition. The thought of being honored at an awards meeting is mouth-watering enough to keep them awake at night. Trophies and certificates remind them of their accomplishments. Offers of congratulation and expressions of admiration confirm for them that they have succeeded. For internal people these things are all quite meaningless. A trophy is nice but not all that important. Internal people get personal satisfaction just knowing they've accomplished something, and knowing they have done well. They don't need the adulation. Much more important to them than the feelings of others is how they feel about themselves.

A Birthday Cake

I learn this psychological information about a representative by asking questions and by being observant. I then use the information to help the salesperson make a "birthday cake."

The idea for the birthday cake goes back to when I was a boy growing up in a family with four brothers. No one got a lot of personal attention. None of us got exactly what we wanted on a daily basis. Except for one day: Your Birthday. On our birthdays our mother would make us any kind of birthday cake we wanted!!! The only limit was your imagination. It could be chocolate with gumdrops. It could be vanilla with banana filling. It could be strawberry with anchovies on it if that was what you wanted.

I attempted to help my salespeople visualize what their "birthday cake" would be like in terms of their lives and our business. It is a process that hits so close to home emotionally that even the most macho representatives have been known to cry. Here is how it would work. An agent and I would be meeting to do goal setting for the coming year. I'd tell the agent, "We are going to make you a 'birthday cake.'" It can be any kind you want; any flavor or color you want; made any way you want it to be made. We are going to make this "birthday cake" for you based on what I know about you and what you know about yourself. If the representative was a "towards pleasure" person I might tell him or her:

> It is December 23, the date of our annual sales dinner. You are sitting in a room at our banquet being honored as one of the people who made it to The Million Dollar Roundtable this year. Your mom and dad, your spouse, your children., your best friend—whomever is important to you—are all there. You know that I am about to tell everyone how well you've done this year. You look around and see all the love and acknowledgement that is there for you. You feel incredibly proud!

If the representative were an "away from" person I might say:

> You've done it. It is December 23, and you know you have made your goal for the year. You now have a portfolio of clients that pretty much guarantees an adequate income for the next several years. You can pay your mortgage without worrying if something breaks down at home you will have the funds to have it fixed. You have enough money to buy the kids the clothes they need. You have savings and you are accumulating money for college tuitions. You are truly supporting your family!

PRINCIPLE 13

External? Internal?

I'd then tell the salesperson to sit there awhile with that image, letting it sink in and become real to him or her. Then I would say, "And all it took for me to do it was"—and they would finish the sentence. The representative would answer the question: How many phone calls do I need to make each day? How many appointments do I need to keep each week? How many open cases do I have to have each month?—and so on. THEY would picture THEIR goal and then arrive at what THEY needed to do to reach it.

The Method

I recommend that each salesperson start every morning with what I call "The Method," which uses the "birthday cake" image to help prepare for the day. "The Method" is a four step process:

(1) Forgiveness: Most successful people are extremely hard on themselves. Every morning a person should forgive himself or herself either for not doing what should have been done the day before, or for doing what should not have been done. A person needs to wipe the slate clean in order to be able to be effective in the new day.

(2) Acknowledgement: A person should also acknowledge that which he or she did well the previous day. People seldom acknowledge the good things they do each day. No matter how trivial it may seem, it is important that we give ourselves a pat on the back.

(3) Affirmation: I believe that in order to orient yourself toward what you want to be in the future you have to state it as if you are already there. Envision yourself as you want to be and then tell yourself that, indeed, that is what you are. For example, "I am a successful,

young sales representative. I have qualified for The Million Dollar Roundtable. I consistently have 20 open cases in inventory. I am proud of what I have accomplished this year in my career."

(4) Visualization: Her is where the "birthday cake" comes into play. You take a few minutes to visualize YOUR cake. You visualize the meaningful results which your good work will bring to you.

"The Method" truly works because it employs the subconscious to help people reach their goals. I taught it to those representatives who wanted to learn it, when they were ready to learn it. The Method can be difficult to stick with. It must become an integral part of a person's daily schedule; whether shortly after awaking, on a morning walk, or sitting in the car before going to the office. It must become a habit. Some people find it hard to start: at times, it may feel silly or awkward. Many people find it difficult to continue; if they suffer a setback they may stop practicing The Method. A manager can be of assistance in these cases. Many people feel it is helpful to check in regularly and report their progress, even if only by leaving a voicemail message

Teaching your salespeople "The Method" for self-motivation is part of treating them as your clients. It is part of doing everything you can to help them succeed.

PRINCIPLE 14
Set Up Incentive Programs that Are Win-Win

Strangely, although our agency did not have awards programs that honored top producers, 82 percent of our agents agreed that, "Our system of honors does a good job of recognizing sales performance." This section outlines a win-win approach to incentives that encourages sales and builds good will throughout an organization.

During my tenure as general agent, I learned that most sales representatives did not enjoy attending luncheons or dinners where they themselves were not being honored. This was especially true if spouses were also in attendance. So, we did away with them. Instead we set up "contests" where the prize was to participate, with family, on an all expenses paid group trip: to Vermont, Disneyworld, Italy, etc. In order to win the contest a representative had to meet his or her individual goal. Every salesperson who met that individual goal won the trip. One agent winning did not prevent another agent from winning. It was a win-win situation without alienating anyone the system works.

I'll explain how it works and why it works. The topics I'll discuss are:

(a) why most everyone dislikes awards dinners
(b) why "top five producers" awards are more discouraging than encougaging
(c) how incentives can be win-win

(d) helping agents set their incentive goals
(e) using "contests" to help them reach their goals.

This is the way it goes at most companies' awards dinners. Several dozen salespeople are sitting around tables with their spouses making small talk. People have a few drinks, and rubber chicken is served. Then the program begins. With some fanfare, it is announced that Joe and Lisa and Tom, are the winners of the top producers awards. Of course, Joe and Lisa and Tom and their families are elated. Meanwhile, every other representative's spouse is eyeing him or her and asking, "Why didn't you get that award?" A few people go home feeling great. Everyone else feels terrible. And, the general manager has spent money hoping that everyone is grateful for the good time the company provided. It just doesn't work.

Like every other sales organization, we held awards dinners every year in my early years as a manager. As we came to understand how much they were hated, we stopped having them. I must point out that it is not just the dinners. It is also the structure of most awards contests, that is, a few people win and everyone else loses. Some may argue that this gives the losers more incentive to work harder. I have found, however, that it does exactly the opposite. After all, only five people can be the top five. Consciously, or subconsciously, most of your salespeople are going to think, "I'm never going to be one of the top five. The agency only seems to care about the top five. Therefore it is hardly worth trying too hard." When we realized this was happening with our representatives, we developed an entirely new approach to sales incentives.

A Win-Win Approach

My grandchildren make fun of the new trend in gym classes at school where the only games that are played are games in

which "everybody wins." However with ou
erybody really did win. The contests were
INDIVIDUAL goals. These goals were set
tween management and the salesperson.
riod a goal was set for each representative
sales in the preceding year (for new associates this method
would vary, but it would still be individually based). To reach
the goal would require that the representative work harder
or smarter than he or she had ever worked before. However,
the goal was attainable and realistic. In keeping with our philosophy that the representatives were our clients, we were
there to help them meet their goal every step of the way.

Typically a majority of our representative would meet their goals set for the contest period. The award: We all would take an agency paid trip together—management and the representatives and their families. Over the years we took some wonderful trips together; from week-end trips to Vermont, to tours of Italy and Spain, to a cruise to Russia. And, every body won. Our representatives boosted their achievement levels and their income; they got to see wonderful, new places; and the representatives bonded with each other. During this "down time," management people and salespeople get to know each other in a more relaxed environment, and the organization receives the benefit of all those increased sales. The "contest" more than pays for itself. Primed by the good time, the salespeople are motivated to try even harder the next time a "contest" is held.

It is not good when your business is reliant on a bunch of "losers." But when awards only go to a top few that is how most of your salespeople are going to feel. However, when incentives are based on a win-win approach everyone feels like a winner. Your salespeople will think of themselves as winners and they will perform like winners.

PRINCIPLE 15
Select Future Managers Based on What They Stand For

This section addresses the selection of second-line managers. A common misconception is that the most successful salespeople will make the best managers. This is not always true. In fact, I would offer that, more commonly, the opposite holds true. That is not to say that a manager shouldn't have sales skills. I caution against using a promotion to management, as a reward for stellar sales results. When selecting people for our management team, I did look at a person's selling skills, but I also sought other qualities. Qualities which, I believe, are more important as relates to a management role. I want to emphasize that simply because a person is not suited for management doesn't mean that he or she isn't a good person. It merely means their talents are better suited to other endeavors.

The items I will cover are:

(a) not everyone is suited for management
(b) qualities to look for in future managers
(c) grooming future managers
(d) how to know when a person is ready for management.

Congratulations! Your business is growing and you need to expand your management team. As you cast about for a new manager, your eye naturally rests on your best sales representatives. Who better to inspire other salespeople and lead them to success? Hold on—not so fast. Not everyone is cut out to be a manager. As a point of fact, the driven, self-starter may be the least likely person to become a coach and a leader.

I've seen it happen: A sales representative has a real knack for connecting with people at point of sale, but it is not a skill he can break down and teach. Successful salespeople-turned-managers may become impatient with others who are not as successful as they are. Top producers may, subconsciously, have a need to be the top gun, which may cause them to, unwittingly, withhold assistance from those they are managing. Super successful people, as a general rule, have a fair amount of ego. It is a part of their makeup that helps to make them as good as they are. However, this is not necessarily a productive management trait.

Four Qualities to Seek Out

New managers should possess four qualities to help them fulfill their mission:

(1) They understand and can teach sales methods. There is a difference between understanding a business's sales methods and actually being successful in using them. Some people have an indefinable talent that enables them to, effortlessly, come across to another human being as trustworthy, competent, and sincere. If a management candidate has this quality, fine. However, it is far more important for him or her to understand what our sales methods are about, and to understand the importance of having new recruits use them. Moreover, the manager must be able to communicate this importance to those folks being supervised.

(2) They must be capable of taking a stand and of defending management actions to fellow representatives.

PRINCIPLE 15

We all have internal compasses which help us determine what is right and wrong and which direction to follow. Some compasses are more finely tuned than others. Picture this—a group of younger salespeople are together, one of them starts complaining about some management policy. The complaining agent is somewhat influential in the group and soon others start to chime in with a "me too" or "you're right." It seems the entire group is in agreement with the dissident's thoughts. Suddenly, one lone representative says that he or she disagrees with the group, This person says, "I understand why management instituted that policy." He or she then makes a case for management's position. Of course, this appeals to me, and most managers, because this representative is endorsing the very policy we believe in. But much more is taking place. It doesn't matter which side is correct. What does matter is that this person has taken a stand among a group of peers. He or she is not afraid to have an opinion that differs from everyone else's opinion. This person is secure enough to think for herself or himself.

(3) They must be philosophically in-tune with your business practices. A member of your management team must fully understand, and be in accord with, the tenets of how you conduct your business. For example, treating the representative as the client; honesty with new recruits; integrity in sales; and so on. Front-line management and second-line management need not always agree, but, if they do not share the same philosophy, they will not be able to work together successfully.

(4) They must derive satisfaction from the successes of others. This trait was the most common characteristic of the management people in our agency. Each of

them sold at one time, some with more success than others. Nevertheless, when they became managers, they had to realize that it was not about them. It was about the the people they were responsible for and the successes of those representatives. Good managers are not in it for the direct thrill of making a big sale or securing a new client. They enjoy the vicarious thrill of having others succeed. A good manager is happiest when salespeople feed back something the manager taught them and the salespeople think they discovered it themselves. The manager's victory lies in the fact that the message got through. When new salespeople enjoy a good relationship with a manager they want to tell that manager about their successes right away; even if it is 10 p.m. Good managers are not annoyed at having been disturbed. In fact, they are thrilled to get that call.

Those who became part of the management team in our agency were schooled in the 22 Principles, normally in Saturday morning sessions where we would examine one principle each session. The message was reinforced for all managers, veteran as well new, at our monthly management meetings. Constant reinforcement of the Principles helps keep everyone on track and working in unison.

PRINCIPLE 16
You Have No Idea of the Impact of What You Say and Do

This section brings out my fundamental belief in the differing expectations a company should have for its sales representatives and its managers. If a sales representative badmouths the business, gets drunk at a company function, or yells at someone in public, you might tolerate it depending on the circumstances. In the same way as you might tolerate those actions by a client. I believe, however, that a manager's behavior must be impeccable. My constant reminder to my management team, and to myself, is, "You have no idea of the impact of what you say and do." My discussion about the importance of managers acting, at all times, as if what they say and do will have a profound impact on their salespeople will address the following points:

(a) why managers' behavior must be beyond reproach
(b) the fact that a manager's words and actions have a impact, positive or negative—when they least expect it
(c) the difficult leap into management—and the part this principle plays in it.

Anyone who has ever been in sales knows that a salesperson puts up with a lot from clients. A client might be rude. It is overlooked. A client may not want to see pictures of your kids—nor is it the client's job to do so. As long as the client is giving the salesperson business, he or she doesn't have to be a favorite person, but he or she will be tolerated.

our agency, as long as they were producing busi-
:speople had a right to do anything that was legal,
..., ... ethical. They could complain all they wanted to whomever would listen. They could badmouth management; they could badmouth the company. They were our clients and their behavior, while not to our liking, would most likely be tolerated. (A side note: This type of behavior tends to repress itself when managers behave impeccably.) Managers, however, were held to a much higher standard. "You have no idea of the impact of what you say and do" was my annoyingly constant reminder to everyone on my team, including myself. And, the most often repeated principle among managers who attended my seminars.

How we conduct ourselves is extraordinarily important to the people around us. They may act cool, sophisticated, and uninterested, but they are watching us like hawks. It took me quite some time to get it fixed in my brain that the things I do—good and bad—can have an unexpected impact on people in general, and my salespeople in particular.

Many years ago, a young agent who had turned in some terrific sales figures in his first five years was invited to speak at our annual agency meeting. This was an honor reserved for a half dozen representatives who had a breakthrough in the past year, or had succeeded despite personal hardship, or had otherwise inspiring stories to relate. This young agent had spoken many tomes about how hard his dad was on him. So, I invited his parents to attend the occasion. After the official ceremonies, I was speaking with Tim and his parents and said, "Aren't you proud of your son." Instead of agreeing, his dad discounted what I had said and denigrated his son with an "It's about time" answer. I was truly annoyed and wanted to put this jerk in his place. But, because of my respect for Tim, I proceeded to tell his father how phenomenal Tim was,

PRINCIPLE 16

and how lucky he was to have Tim for a son. I never gave a thought to the effect of my words on Tim. Years later he told me it was one of the most important moments of his life. I can now look back and see that that meeting marked a turning point for him. His loyalty to the agency, and to me, from that point on was something to behold. And, because he felt supported, he changed from a slightly self-centered nice guy to one of the true givers in the agency. Today, he is deeply respected and extremely successful; and, he has a better relationship with his father.

You Have No Idea of The Impact of Your Actions

That was a good thing I did with Tim. My words and actions had a positive impact. On the other hand, I've come close to losing some of the best people in my organization by not being conscious of what I, the titular head of the organization, was saying or doing. That almost happened with a buddy who had helped me build the agency from three to, at that time, nearly a hundred agents. We were good friends. We also had genuine disagreements about issues affecting the agency. Normally we would go out to lunch to iron out our disagreements. This particular day, however, he did something that really annoyed me. Without thinking, I went down the hall and began berating him in front of a group of people. The next morning he came roaring into my office and said, "If you ever do that again, I'm out of here." I was shocked! I didn't even realize I had embarrassed him. That day I almost lost a dear friend because I hadn't thought about the impact of what I said, and did. However, I did learn a valuable lesson about the importance and the impact of what I say and do.

Things that you say and do may affect people's lives in ways you may never know about. A few years ago, one of our most talented young representatives received a prestigious award: lifetime membership in the Million Dollar Roundtable. This is a huge achievement. The following week, in a sales meeting, after I had complimented him on the award, he turned to one of our senior associates, Dick Wilsey, and said, "You know Dick, I have that award because of you." Dick was quite surprised. The young man explained, "When I first joined the agency, I saw that plaque in your office. Then and there I decided I wanted it. I wanted to be the kind of person who reaches that level of achievement." Dick had no idea of the impact of what he had done—which was to earn that plaque and display it proudly.

Managers must be aware that every time they sit with a representative and give advice, it has to be the best they can give. That bit of advice can possibly turn around someone's life. I remember a situation in the mid 1980s. We had hired a group of pretty sharp young guys who, however, were not ready to really be serious about their work. They were out a lot sowing their oats. Eventually, most of them got serious and their careers started to take off. The guy with the most talent, however, was still fooling around: out drinking four nights a week, dating several women, and partying hearty. Nevertheless, I really liked him. After a sales builder, in which I had been particularly tough on him, I called him into my office, and told him, "You know I'm a fun guy, and when I started I didn't take the business too seriously. But, the reason I'm hard on you now is that the train has left the station and your buddies are on it. If you don't make some changes, they're not going to have too much time for you. You see, people tend to associate with others who have the same belief structure. Once that train has gone much farther, you won't be able to run and catch it." Of course he was quite upset and angry with me. In fact he went home and put his fist through a wall. But, he had listened, and he began to notice what his friends were doing. He realized they were

PRINCIPLE 16

moving away from him, and decided that he was on the wrong track. Well, almost overnight, his production level and level of seriousness changed. Everything changed. He stopped the excessive partying and running around. He began dating a wonderful woman, and subsequently married her. Today, if he notices some guy or girl at the agency heading down the wrong path tells that story. When I had that conversation, I had no idea whether or not it would have any impact on him. I really went into it to justify my being hard on him, as much as to benefit him. You really cannot know the impact of what you say and do.

Negativism Is So Detrimental

Anything negative a manager has to say about an organization is, potentially, very disturbing to those folks being supervised, and it can cause them to become uncomfortable about their jobs. Furthermore, if one manager is in open disagreement with another, e.g. telling the salespeople something that is contradictory to what other managers are saying, it creates confusion, uneasiness, and fear among the salespeople. It causes them to wonder about the organization and about what they themselves are doing. It also gives them an opportunity to pit one manager against another (just as kids will do with mom and dad). And, it enables them to rationalize their own errors by blaming the inconsistency of the managers

Transitioning Into Management

The transition from being one of the gang to being a manager is not an easy one. Whenever someone joins our management team, even on a part-time basis, I attempt to forewarn him or her. I say, "This will be a wonderful, new experience, but, there is some bittersweetness to it. The good part is that you're entering a new world where people work together on a fun and harmonious basis. This should give you a great deal of satisfaction. It's a wonderful experience being part of this management team. The hard part is, you've changed roles. No matter how small a part you play in management, you now represent the agency in everything, good or bad, that you say or do. You must honor that from now on. The way you present yourself is far more important now because you are representing the agency. You may even have to change or discontinue relationships you have with other salespeople—maybe those you have been friends with for several years. Prior to now you have had the right to bitch about the job. Now, if you want to complain, you've got to complain to us and only to us, the management team. You lose the right to do otherwise."

Managers must help each other with this principle. It is important that we each know the effect that our actions have on the people we manage. As salespeople, we are naturally aware of what we say and do in front of clients. As managers, we must be consciously aware of what we say and do in front of our sales representatives, our clients.

Do you have any idea of the impact of what you say and do? It is one of the most important tools we have in our efforts to help our salespeople do a better job.

PRINCIPLE 17
Avoid Triangular Relationships (Like the Plague)

Triangular relationships are the bane of office life. A triangular relationship occurs when Person A has a problem with Person B and deals with it by telling Person C. Triangular relationships, however, never solve any problems. I maintain their aim is to create resentment and discord. One of my unalterable tenets is that, particularly where managers are involved, triangular relationships are always to be avoided. Whenever a manager or agent came to me to complain about someone else in the agency, my invariable response was, "And what did they say when you told them that?". This section explores the problem of triangular relationships as well as how to dismantle triangles and the positive effect of eliminating them.

The topics covered are:

(a) what is a triangular relationship
(b) what is its purpose
(c) why they must nor be tolerated
(d) how to immediately dismantle them
(e) why triangular relationships that don't involve managers are not as detrimental.

Why am I so concerned about triangular relationships? Triangles are supposed to be very stable. Perhaps that is so for stools and tables. In business, however, triangular relationships and triangular situations are among the worst things that can happen to morale and motivation.

As mentioned above, a triangle occurs when Person A has a problem with Person B, and, rather than address the problem directly with B, A complains to Person C. At first glance this doesn't seem so bad. Maybe there is a reason why A does not want to confront B. Maybe A needs some support and C is very sympathetic. What's wrong with that? What is wrong is that triangular relationships never solve problems. In reality they prolong them and cause them to fester. They breed secrets and resentment, which erode morale and motivation. For these reasons they can never be tolerated in business. An example: Jerry, a sales representative, does not feel that his district manager, Ellen. is supporting him in his sales efforts. Jerry, however, does not bring his concerns directly to Ellen. Instead, he brings it up with his sales trainer, Jim. He approaches Jim and says, "Ellen is not really doing anything to help me." Jerry may be even less direct. Often triangular situations star with a compliment: "Jim, you have always been so supportive of me. I wish Ellen were more like you." Jerry is appealing to Jim's ego. If Jim is not as alert about triangular relationships as a manager should be, he may be flattered by Jerry's confidences. Where might the conversation go from there? Perhaps, in an effort to be sympathetic, Jim might say a few derogatory things about Ellen. What has happened? Jim, a member of the management team, has aligned himself against another member of the team. A very bad, and potentially explosive, situation has been created. There is one key criterion by which to judge whether this whole situation has been beneficial or detrimental: has it solved the problem? The answer is a resounding "NO."

In fact, what has occurred is the sowing of the seeds of discontent and mistrust. If this is not nipped in the bud, the result will be a growing distrust and an erosion of morale amongst the sales force. If the practice is allowed to continue it will surely spread and become insidious.

PRINCIPLE 17

It is my experience that sales representatives try to create these triangular relationships when they are not doing their jobs. Creating these situations is often an attempt to deflect attention away from their shortcomings.

What To Do

I trained our managers to listen attentively and respectfully and then ask the question,"What did Ellen say when you told her that?" The common response is, "Well I have not told her." The manager must then suggest that the proper way to deal with the situation is for Jerry to speak directly to Ellen. The manager should also point out the positive effect that the direct approach will have for the representative, for Ellen, and for the agency in general. It may take a few such incidences, but eventually the sales representative will realize the futility of his or her actions. He or she will recognize that the management team is a cohesive, unified group The awareness of that unity will have a positive impact, not only on that salesperson, but on the rest of the sales force as well Moreover, the direct approach will bring about positive feelings among the members of the management team. A strong team will become even stronger. Truly a win-win result.

I also disliked triangular relationships among the sales representatives. Those types of relationships are just not healthy. However, I am not as wary of those situations which don't involve management. I would, most often, allow them to work themselves out. Nevertheless, if I felt that agency morale was being affected, I would promptly step in and try to resolve the problem. And, if the triangular relationship involved management I would put a stop to it immediately. I cannot over-emphasize the importance of eliminating such triangular situations.

An added benefit is that the sales representatives stop trying to play these games. They catch themselves and back down: "You're going to ask me what he said when I told him, right?" Curing the representatives of this habit allows them to become more up front with themselves about their responsibilities in the manager-sales representative relationship. And, it clears the way for managers to be of assistance to the best of their ability. Managers are better able to treat the representatives as valued clients.

PRINCIPLE 18
Get the Monkeys Off Your Back

I learned the lesson of this principle the hard way. The principle I'm referring to is delegating authority and responsibility. It is an understatement to say that I had to work at learning to delegate. By nature, I am a problem solver. Unfortunately that trait can lead to a person trying to solve everyone's problems for them. Not a good business practice; in fact, a potential pitfall for a manager.

In this section the points I will cover are:

(a) where the monkeys come from
(b) the problem with having too many monkeys
(c) how to "pass the monkey back"
(d) allowing managers and other key people to do their jobs.

Many years ago, I read an article in a business journal that really changed the way I thought about delegating. It went something like this: Assume you are a newly appointed manager. You want to make a good impression on the people in the office. You want to show them what a good boss you will be. An associate, Al, comes to your office and tells you, "I have a problem and I can't figure out how to solve it." He then describes his problem to you. You, of course want to help. So, you say, "Let me give it some thought." Al says, "Great," he leaves. What you had not thought about was that when Al came in he had a "monkey" on his back. What happened when you agreed to think about it was that he took the monkey off his back and put it on yours. Now you have the monkey and Al leaves, his load a little lighter. Okay, you have one monkey. No big deal you can handle it. Then, Liz comes into your office. She says, "I had a terrible problem with a client. I've had this same problem for several weeks. I can't seem to get rid of it." Naturally you want to be a good manager for Liz also. You say, "Liz you are a good saleswoman, you work very hard, let me see if I can straighten that out." Liz is very thankful and she leaves. Well, Liz also had a monkey on her back which has now been transferred to your back. Now you have two! But you can handle them, right? Shortly thereafter Armando comes in and says, "I've got some real problems." You know the scenario I'm creating. You accept another monkey.

You Cannot Be Present

Shortly thereafter, Rachel comes into your office and begins to tell you what a good week she is having. But you can't hear a word she is saying because those monkeys are scratching at your head. You can't pay attention to her good news. You have loaded yourself up with monkeys that are demanding your attention. Al, Liz, and Armando think you're a hero, but the truth is you have not helped anyone. You are so overburdened with monkeys that you can't even hear Rachel. You are unable to be present with this representative, your client. And not a single problem has been solved.

Give The Monkey Back

I truly recognized myself in that anecdote. I had allowed the same thing to happen to me too many times, until I was forced to come up with a solution. My solution was to give the monkey back. Anyone who came into my office with a

PRINCIPLE 18

problem was given an assignment. Not a minor, meaningless assignment. A major, meaningful assignment. I had different strategies for different problems. For example, assume Dan came in to talk to me about the problem he was having upgrading his client's policies. I'd say, "Here is what I want you to do: I want you to go through last year's records and make a list of everyone you called on. Write down their incomes and the policy levels you feel you should have gotten them to but didn't. When the list is completed call me and we will meet to discuss those you have concerns about." If someone was concerned about her rate of referrals from clients, I'd refer her to our sales tape dealing with that problem. I'd tell her, "Listen to the tape and try to apply the lessons to your situation. Then come back to me and we will talk about how you did." If someone complained that his client's application for insurance was being turned down by the underwriter, I'd ask him to read the underwriting manual to see if we could justify the risk to the company. Let me be very clear that I was not putting those salespeople off with busy work. I was giving them legitimate and practical steps to take to solve their problems. I was making sure that what was their problem did not become solely my problem. By giving back the monkey I made the representative—not me—the prime mover on the problem.

The end results of passing the monkey back were all beneficial. If the salesperson didn't come back it meant that the problem either was solved or wasn't really that important. Moreover, any assignment given resulted in expanding the representative's knowledge. Most important, I freed myself to be present for all my "clients."

Let Your Associates Do Their Jobs

There is another aspect related to delegating which applies to many managers. For some managers it isn't enough to take on everyone else's monkeys. They also feel they have to help their representatives and their staff do their jobs—even if those people are not having any problems. I was also guilty of this error. I learned, the hard way, to stop being that way.

When our agency was just getting started, our office manager, Glenda, was constantly annoyed at me for second-guessing some of her decisions. Those decisions involved everything from the Christmas decorations to associates' vacation schedules; little things?—and big things?—micro-managing? Glenda decided to teach me a lesson. Whenever anyone came to her with a question or a problem, she would send him or her to me. After all I was the one with all the answers right? After a few days of having to make all the decisions that Glenda was perfectly capable of making on her own, I smartened up and got the message. Let Glenda do her job!!

Enable Don't Disable

If you give a person the responsibility of doing a job for you, you must trust them. You must enable them to do their job, even though they may not do it the way you would. If you do not have confidence in them, they will lose confidence in themselves. If you are constantly second-guessing them, they lose the ability and the desire to take charge of things and to make decisions. If people are to be held accountable and responsible for getting a job done, the must be given the freedom to do that job to the best of their abilities.

As I progressed in my career and learned to give the "monkeys" back, I resolved only to involve myself in problems where I was absolutely needed. I call it the "last 10 percent."

PRINCIPLE 18

My management team and established representatives knew that I had confidence in them but that I was there for them if they really needed me. An interesting aside, when asked what they liked about working with me, many members of our team replied "He lets me do my job." It felt good to be told that.

PRINCIPLE 19
Set Attainable Goals as an Organization

Just as with any individual, every business endeavor must set attainable goals for itself. Without attainable goals to strive for, stagnation of that business is inevitable. I firmly believe that if a business stops growing it begins dying; and, without goals, growth does not occur. I also believe that, whereas a goal must be realistic, it must require a concerted and unified effort to be meaningful.

In this section I'll discuss:

(a) why every business needs goals
(b) establishing attainable goals
(c) getting "buy-in"
(d) celebrating the attainment of goals
(e) what to do if a goal is not reached.

A Little History

Back in the 1960s, I was a member of a study group made up of Northwestern district managers. We were a bunch of aggressive young bucks from different markets sharing strategies for success. To help promote discussion, we decided to come up with a goal we could all have in common. A goal that each of us would answer to each time we met. One member of the group, from Florida, suggested that each of us should strive to dominate the marketplace in our respective geographic areas. Each of us stated individual goals related to that master goal. Mine were to:

(1) have the largest life insurance agency in Fairfield County, Conn.
(2) have the highest rate of productivity per producer
(3) have my salespeople be financially well off. I did not want to reign over mediocrity. I wanted my producers to be people who had "made it"—a tall order in our affluent area of the country
(4) have my competition be salespeople who had not made it with our organization.

Pretty cocky, if you ask me! But, by the early 1970s, when I became a general agent, we had reached those goals. We did dominate our marketplace. Our sales force was incredibly productive, Our agency had overcome the "80-20 rule," which says that 80 percent of a sales organization's production normally comes from the top 20 percent of its producers. We had, to use a sports phrase, a "deep bench."

At that point our business hit a malaise. We slowed down considerably. I wasn't as excited about what I was doing. The agency's growth was sluggish and we were beginning to stagnate. We had lost focus. I then contracted with an outside consulting group to help us regain our enthusiasm, and get back on track. They met and talked with just about everyone in the agency. Ultimately, they gave us some very good scores on most of the things we were doing. Their one negative comment was that we had lost our sense of mission. We had achieved what we set out to achieve in much less time than we thought it would take. We were, essentially, without goals and were drifting. If we didn't know where we wanted to go, how could we possibly get there?

PRINCIPLE 19

Back to the drawing board! Our entire management team spent a great deal of time talking about, and thinking about, our goals. Where did we want to go and why? What was our mission? We finally came up with "The Pursuit of Excellence" (several years before the best selling book of that title), and the criteria for that pursuit. We realized that we could not simply "be" excellent: we must constantly be striving for excellence. This new focus and our criteria for it carried us forward over the next few decades.

Moving Forward

Each year we would establish an annual goal for the agency. A goal which helped us to continue our "pursuit of excellence." This goal would be attainable only if everyone recognized that it could be reached. And, we all realized that reaching the goal would require a concerted effort by each of us to reach our individual goals. Only then could the sum be greater than the total of the parts. Getting "buy-in" to this concept was critical to the health of the agency. The first step in getting overall buy-in was to have every member of the management team buy in. Management had to embrace the goal, believe in the goal, and be committed to the goal. If not, the sales force would not be committed to it, and it would not be reached. The next step was to put in place a plan for reaching the goal. A workable, realistic plan leading to success. Then, we would communicate the goal to everyone in the agency. We would point out that each producer meeting his or her individual goals contributed to the agency meeting its goal. And, we would illustrate how our agency goal fit within the framework of our "pursuit of excellence."

Monitoring and Reinforcing

During the year we would continuously monitor each salesperson's progress towards individual goals, as well as the agency's progress towards its goal. The entire agency would be kept up to date as to where the agency stood in relationship to its goal, and, as to what remained to be done in order to reach it. Each checkpoint provided an opportunity to reiterate and reinforce our commitment to the goal, and the importance of attaining it. Each milestone reached was a cause for celebration of everyone's efforts. And, of course, achieving the annual goal resulted in an agency-wide celebration; perhaps a large family party, or a trip. A pre-established reward that we all could share.

Falling Short

As noted above, I believe a goal must be attainable. But, to be meaningful, the attainment of the goal must require aiming high and extending ourselves. There were years when we did not hit our goal. There could be many reasons for failing to do so. We would deal with these failures openly, try to figure out why we didn't make, and get back to trying again. Perhaps we had set the goal too high; if so that was acceptable. Hopefully, we had never set it too low. If you are achieving your goals without great effort, watch out. It is said that the most dangerous miles on a trip are the final few before reaching your destination. Don't let your guard down. Don't become complacent. Set a new goal, knowing the steps you will have to take to reach it, and get back to work.

Whenever I think about setting a goal too high, I remind myself of 1961, when President Kennedy announced the goal of putting a man on the moon by the end of the decade. He was (literally) shooting for the moon. In response to his

PRINCIPLE 19

challenge, our space agency, NASA, embraced the goal and went after it. The agency made extraordinary achievements over the next eight years and reached their goal. A source of great pride and celebration for the entire nation. Did our president aim too high? Evidentally not.

Make it Enjoyable

Setting goals, and striving to reach them, should be an enjoyable experience for you and your sales team. The entire process can be, and should be, fun for everyone. It will be if you, the leader, make it so.

PRINCIPLE 20
Have No Secrets Among Management

There was not one salesperson in our agency who didn't believe that when he or she was talking to one member of the management team, he, or she was talking to the entire management team. It was common knowledge that there were no secrets among our managers. This principle helps make any business a place where the priority is production not politics. Moreover, this principle creates a sense of harmony and security among the sales representatives because they need not worry about petty office politics.

The points covered in this section are:

(a) why managers should have no secrets
(b) production reigns over politics
(c) no secrets vs. no triangles
(d) how far does "no secrets" go
(e) the painful side of telling secrets
(f) sales representatives get the message.

A cardinal rule for any management team should be not to keep secrets from each other. This rule helps to maintain a tremendous sense of unity among managers as well as ensuring that no manager seeks to put himself or herself above any other manager. This sense of unity generates a positive feeling of stability and security for the entire organization; and most especially, for the sales force.

Example

Assume Tim, a member of the management team, is approached by Jenna, a sales representative. Jenna is having a great deal of trouble; she really needs help. In fact, she is considering resigning. Tim promises to help her, as would any good manager. But, what happens if Tim keeps this to himself and does not tell any of the other members of the management team? Well, first of all, it is a loss to Jenna. Jenna may get the benefit of Tim's attention but she will miss the opportunity to get support and encouragement from the rest of the management team. Another member of the team might not necessarily get directly involved in helping her, but an extra friendly "hello," or some reassurance that these things have happened to other representatives who have gone on to success may be missed. These little extra expressions of support can be invaluable. And they can also let Jenna know she needn't be ashamed or try to hide what she is experiencing from the other managers.

Tim's keeping Jenna's problem a secret from the rest of the managers has another unfortunate consequence. It is the consequence of Tim setting himself apart from the rest of the management team. By keeping a secret, Tim has begun to weaken the strength of the entire team, which is harmful to the entire organization.

Our managers shared with each other everything that went on in the agency. We were constantly in communication with each other. As a last resort, our monthly management meetings provided an opportunity for open discussion.

No Secrets vs. No Triangles

In a way the "no secrets" principle might be seen as violating the "no triangles" principle. Suppose Jenna's problem

PRINCIPLE 20

involved Peter, another manager. What Tim should do, and would do, is encourage Jenna to speak directly to Peter. But, what if Jenna refused? If Peter were another associate, and not a manager, Tim might let it go. However, because Peter is a member of the management team, Tim has an obligation to tell Peter what is going on. Tim, if he cannot persuade Jenna to go directly to Peter, must inform Jenna that he is going to talk with Peter and explain why he is doing so. Otherwise, by keeping silent, he is tacitly agreeing with what Jenna has said. He has taken sides with Jenna against Peter, a member of the team.

Production vs. Politics

A tenet of our organization was that production took precedence over politics. I did my very best to curtail and wipe out petty office politics. In my opinion, petty office politics are just that, petty. I believe they are divisive and detrimental to an entire culture. I cannot think of a single positive aspect of office politics. An environment of "secrets" spawns office politics that adversely affects production. Also, that type of environment, generally, leads to cliques and "special" groups. Not a good situation for any business. And, certainly not good for a business which is trying to grow and prosper.

How Far Does "No Secrets" Go???

This is an extremely difficult question to answer. Whereas the rule is no secrets, there will be that one situation that severely tests a manager. A situation where the manager is fearful that, by not keeping something secret, the representative or the representative's family will be harmed. Perhaps the matter discussed is so sensitive that revealing it will be detrimental to everyone. I caution you that these situations should be few and far between. Furthermore, a manager must do everything he, or she, can do to avoid them. If put into that type of situation, a manager must be guided by his, or her, personal value system.

The Message Gets Out

How do the representatives know we didn't harbor secrets? They learned very quickly, either from a manager telling them, or from other representatives telling them, or the hard way, personal experience The members of your sales force talk to each other about virtually everything that occurs in your business. They have their own network. I repeat, there wasn't one salesperson in our organization who didn't believe that when he or she was talking to one member of the management team, he or she was talking to the entire team. This awareness can change the manager/representative dynamic. If a representative is telling a manager something and he or she knows that he or she is talking to the whole management team, the tendency is to discuss the problem while omitting the personal feelings attached to it. Personally, I think that is fine. The manager can avoid some unpleasant conversation and just work on solving the problem. A win-win situation.

Yay! Team

The basis of "no secrets" is that management is a team. A team works together towards a common goal. One member of the team does not enhance himself or herself by stepping on another member. As the popular saying goes, one member doesn't "throw another member under the bus."

A final thought, share this principle with others, don't keep it a secret.

PRINCIPLE 21
Management Should Work by Consensus

What is the best way for a management team to make decisions about the operation of their business? After several years of being exposed to various methods, from autocracy to democracy, I discovered the vast benefits of having a management team operate by consensus.

This chapter explores the advantages and disadvantages of different systems of decision making; and, why consensus is the best system for moving an organization forward with unity of purpose. It outlines the specific mechanics I and my managers found worked best to facilitate consensus. It also recommends ways of dealing with consensus's few drawbacks—including the time it takes to arrive at a decision.

This section will address:

(a) why consensus is best
(b) the problems with other methods of decision making
(c) the mechanics of consensus
(d) setting meeting agendas
(e) tabling decisions
(f) moderating and promoting discussion
(g) reaching consensus
(h) consensus and time management.

Most people associate management by consensus with ineficiency; with long hours debating very small points;

and, with people who have too much time on their hands. When they hear that the management team in our agency operated by consensus, they think we must have been crazy. Nevertheless, we managed by consensus for three decades and never regretted it. We found that the unifying process of working by consensus was an incredible force in moving our organization forward. The positive aspects of this unity far outweighed any negatives associated with the consensus process. With the weight of the management team behind every decision there was no one putting on the brakes. Consensus was not a drag on our business; it was an empowering force!

When I started in management, I called myself a benevolent dictator. I believed that the buck stopped at my desk, and, while I would respect all opinions, I reserved the right to make all decisions by my authority alone. As time passed, however, I didn't use my power to overrule my managers. The more I worked with the team the less I was in charge—and the better our organization became. Consensus was taking hold, and we were better for it

Monthly Management Meetings

Our monthly management meetings (see Principle 22) were conducted on the basis of consensus. Attending these meetings were our district managers; agents with managerial responsibilities; and salaried employees, such as our office manager, who were integral to running the agency. A total of about twelve people. A management team of this size can only be effective if it operates by consensus. Here is how we worked. The agenda was set by everyone. Anyone with a topic to be discussed listed it on a white board. The goal for the meeting was to cover everything on that board. Needless to say, that didn't always happen. Asterisks were put beside

PRINCIPLE 21

those items that had to be decided that day. Agenda items could, and did, include everything from A to Z. Although I facilitated all the management meetings, discussion of a particular topic was led by the person listing it for discussion. Every topic got an airing. Discussion took place in an atmosphere of respect. Everyone with a stake in the matter got to have his or her say, without anyone being dismissive or scornful. Each of us knew that mutual respect was key to our being successful.

By the end of our hours of meeting together, one of three things took place:

(1) a consensus decision had been reached on that agenda item
(2) two or three people had agreed to research the topic and have more information for our next meeting
(3) the group agreed to table the item for the next meeting.

Unlike a jury, we did not necessarily require unanimity on all matters. Some decisions could not be put off; for those, if we hadn't reached a consensus, majority would rule. Everyone was united behind those decisions because we knew that we had all been heard on the matter, and it was important to move forward.

The more difficult decisions that were not urgent might be carried forward from meeting to meeting. I recall one of the most difficult issues we had to deal with. It involved making the agents responsible for allowing policies they had sold to lapse prematurely. Our parent company began imposing monetary penalties on the general manager for lapsed policies. Most general managers began passing those penalties on to the agents responsible for the lapsed policies. We, on the other hand, did not like acting punitively towards the sales force. Initially, we declined to impose the penalties on the salespeople.

However, we found that the lapse rates in those agencies where the penalties had been imposed were going down; but, ours were staying the same. The members of our management team had strong opinions, pro and con, as to whether we should also start imposing those penalties. We discussed this dilemma over about six meetings without reaching a consensus. Finally, one member of our team suggested a compromise whereby the agents were given several opportunities to rectify their mistakes before a penalty would be imposed. A compromise on which we did reach consensus. It was pure torture to discuss this issue from meeting to meeting. I was strongly tempted to step in and put a stop to it, and to decide the matter based only on what I thought. But, I didn't, and the final decision was owned by everyone because everyone had put so much effort into reaching that decision.

Sometimes It Takes Time

Did we spend a lot of time and effort and energy on that issue? You bet we did. Was it worth it? You bet it was!! It was an example of our firm belief that we were a team, and that we operated by consensus. If they hadn't known it before, every member of the team now knew that their opinions were important and respected. In addition, each member of the team could tell every salesperson they supervised that the matter had been discussed in depth before a decision was made. And, that management was unified in support of that decision.

Visitors to our meetings found them to be maddeningly informal. They said we were all over the place and without a fixed regimen. They couldn't believe that we didn't cut

PRINCIPLE 21

discussion short. Well, that might all have been true. Decision making by consensus does take more time. But I can unequivocally tell you that it is worth it.

Tension vs. Tension

In every organization, there are two types of tension that work against each other: relationship tension and task tension.

RELATIONSHIP TENSION

———————————————→

TASK TENSION

←———————————————

Relationship tension is the amount of conflict involved in your dealings with others. Task tension is the amount of energy that is devoted to a task. When relationship energy is high, it consumes a lot of energy. On the other hand, the more you are able to reduce relationship energy, the more energy you can devote to your task: building a successful sales force.

How do you reduce relationship tension? By building trust. By doing what you say you are going to do. By listening to and taking into account the opinions of others. By seeking and building consensus.

"Think and Grow Rich"

More than 70 years ago, during the Great Depression, a newspaper reporter named Napoleon Hill wrote a whopper of a best seller titled titled, "Think and Grow Rich." The book contained the wisdom he gleaned from interviewing 504 of the country's richest men. Although it seems incredibly old fashioned reading the book today, it has been one of my inspirations. Not necessarily the "Grow Rich" aspect, though there's nothing wrong with that. Rather, it is Hill's advice about thinking: thinking about how to achieve success.

One of the most innovative ideas in his book is one he attributes to Andrew Carnegie, namely the "master mind" concept. He defines it as "coordination of knowledge and effort, in a spirit of harmony, between two or more people for the attainment of a definite purpose," and Hill says, "No two minds ever come together without, thereby, creating a third invisible, intangible force which may be likened to a third mind."

If two minds can do that much, think what a dozen minds are capable of achieving. However, the only way a dozen minds can come together, with a shared definite purpose, is by working through consensus. I wholeheartedly believe the energy generated within our management team, by us working together on a consensus basis, gave us the ability to move our business forward in a way no group of people at odds with each other could ever have achieved.

PRINCIPLE 22
Management Meetings Are Sacred

If in keeping no secrets, and deciding by consensus, managers are thinking as one mind, they must also, in their actions outside management meetings, act as one body. Managers must not share, with non-team members, anything that is discussed in a management meeting. This rule applies equally to matters of great and small importance. Only when the team itself has decided "what, when, how, and to whom" may the information then be shared with others.

This section discusses:

(a) why management discussions must be limited to team members
(b) the "sacredness" of management meetings
(c) trust
(d) unity
(e) the effectiveness of team action.

In our agency, management meetings were sacred. What does that mean? One thing that means is that a member did not miss a meeting unless he or she was sick or there had been a death in the family. Attendance at the meetings was of the highest priority.

Our management meetings were held once a month. We would get together, briefly, between regular meetings if something came up which required a decision. Regular monthly meetings dealt with immediate issues as well as with long-range planning.

During management meetings, interruptions were not allowed. We did not take phone calls, except, of course, urgent family matters. Cell phones were turned off. Everyone was prepared to stay as long as needed. We started at 1 p.m. and ended at about 5 or 6 p.m. or sometimes 7 p.m. Afterward, those managers whose income was dependent on production, i.e. non-salaried members, would have dinner together, to socialize and to discuss issues that only affected those of us in that situation.

In addition to our monthly meetings, in January and June, we met off-site for three days. Everyone arrived on time and stayed overnight. The January meeting involved planning for the year ahead; the June meeting was to assess where we stood in relation to our goals, and to make adjustments as needed. Both meetings began with a discussion of relationship issues. Each manager took as much time as he or she needed to describe what was happening in their lives. Everyone talked about what was going well for them, as well as what problems they might be facing. If someone was having problems, the team helped explore what was going on and attempted to offer possible solutions. This practice reduced relationship tension and allowed us to focus on the tasks ahead of us. It is worthy of repetition to say that nothing that was discussed at management meetings was discussed with anyone other than members of the management group. (Spouses were an exception, but only if a member knew that a spouse was not going share what was said with anyone else.)

PRINCIPLE 22

Trust and Unity

One of the main reasons for the no-discussion rule is the all important matter of trust. If a person can trust that others won't repeat what has been said, he or she will feel free to speak his or her mind. We valued and respected all points of view, and we wanted open and unrestricted discussions. Another valuable aspect of the no-discussion rule is that it allows management to present a united front.

Example: Imagine that the management team has made a decision that may be unpopular with some of the sales representatives. Assume that a representative comes to you, a manager, and complains about the decision. Assume further that you respond, "Well I didn't think it was such a good idea but everyone else did." You may have scored a few points with that representative but you have undercut the authority of the management team. You've made it less likely that the representative will accept that decision. And, ultimately, you have made that representative feel less secure. A management team must always present a united front. To do otherwise erodes trust, and reduces the effectiveness of management decisions.

We had very little tolerance for anyone who took management discussions outside the meetings. If someone did that once, the guilty party was reminded of the trust issue. And, was told again how such an action hurt the management team, as well as the entire organization. If that person violated the principle a second time he or she was off the management team. That is how important this principle was to us.

Management must be a team and must act as a team. When we made a decision all stood by that decision and took ownership of it. Working as a team helps reinforce management's efforts to assist the sales force. Uniformity of management's message makes it more effective.

Management is effective only insofar as it acts as a team. And building the team are what management meetings are all about!!

TRANSFERABILITY

Earlier in this book, I stated that I would relate another example of the transferability of the 22 Principles. This example involves me personally.

In September of 2002, I retired as general agent for Northwestern Mutual. Shortly thereafter I began paying increasing attention to a company in which I am the majority shareholder. This business is a property and casualty insurance agency. I have been an owner of this company since the mid 1970s. Because of my duties at Northwestern, I had paid only nominal attention to that business.

The property/casualty insurance business is very different than the life insurance business, and was quite foreign to me. At that time I knew very little about the workings of the "P and C" business. It is safe to say I know only marginally more about the business today. But I do know how to manage a sales organization. I became more and more involved in overseeing the management of the agency. I welcomed the opportunity to, once again, put the 22 Principles to the test.

Over the years, the agency had done well, growing at a respectable rate. By 2005 the agency was quite large, and was well respected by its peers, and by the property/casualty insurers. In early 2005, I gave myself and the managers of the agency a challenge: "Let's double the production of the agency in five years." Mind you, this was already a "going" business. Doubling it in size in five years presented a daunting task. The goal seemed unrealistic and unreachable. Nevertheless, we all agreed to accept the challenge.

We put together the "2010" plan. A four-point plan to accomplish the task we had set for ourselves. And, we went to work. An integral part of our approach was applying the principles outlined in these pages to the management of the agency, Starting, of course, with the principle that the "sales representatives are our clients."

At the time of this writing we are almost 18 months into the five year plan. I am thrilled to tell you the Principles are working. We are substantially ahead of target at this point in time. I have no doubt we will reach our goal!

The Principles are indeed transferable!!

AFTERWORD

Well, there you have it. My 22 Principles for Success in Building and Maintaining a Dynamic Sales Force.

I am well aware that there are other methods of managing a sales force. I have known many managers who think their role is to beat performance out of their salespeople. That might be a road to success; but it is also a road to misery. There is another way—a better way. Treat your representative as your clients. Respect them and treat them well. Work as a team with other managers. Follow the 22 Principles, they will not fail you.

I repeatedly tell managers who seek my counsel, "There are many ways of being successful. But, what I can teach you that others can't is how to have JOY in your career. How to do it is simple—follow the principles."

The Principles represent the ideal, and I have failed at every one of them many, many times. But, I held true to them and they have had their effect. As a result, I've developed lasting, satisfying relationships; I've made a lot of money; and, I did not have to kill myself doing it. Starting early in my management career, I have taken a minimum of three months vacation every year. I've been able to travel the world. I have visited more than 100 countries, and I have been privileged to personally experience the goodness of people everywhere.

The reason I have been able to do these things is that I knew my job. I never missed a wedding, funeral, or graduation.

I attended every sales meeting. And I was always available to my representatives when they needed me. I never forgot that the representatives were my clients. I worked with a management "team," not just a group of managers. A team of people who, I was sure, would adhere to the 22 Principles even though I might not be physically present.

The joy of management for me has been watching people grow; observing how, with nurturing and nourishing, they became better performers and better people. Young men and women who joined our organization right out of school have grown up, married and had children they are able to raise in comfort. They've become responsible members of our community and the communities in which they live. Career changers, who were extremely unhappy in their jobs, have joined us and turned their lives around. These are the things that are meaningful in my life.

Thanks to the 22 Principles my career has been, and still is, a wonderful and joyous life experience.

I offer you the 22 Principles with the sincerest belief they can do the same for you.

AUTHOR'S NOTE

The Principles outlined in this book were developed and formulated during my more than 40 years managing salespeople. My experiences have not come out of a theoretical experiment; they have come out of the real day-to-day world of business. I an eternally grateful to those people who have mentored me, and from whom I have learned.

I am especially grateful to those sales representatives, my clients, who have enriched my life and brought me joy. I will not attempt to list their names for fear I might forget someone.

To each and every one of them I say:

THANK YOU

Made in the USA